White Woods, Quiet Trails

A GUIDE TO

CROSS-COUNTRY SKIING,

BACKCOUNTRY TREKS

& SNOWSHOE OUTINGS

IN AND AROUND

LAKE SUPERIOR'S SAWTOOTH

MOUNTAINS

**Exploring Minnesota's
North Shore in Winter**

Andrew Slade

RIDGELINE PRESS
TWO HARBORS, MINNESOTA

White Woods, Quiet Trails:
Exploring Minnesota's North Shore in Winter
A guide to cross-country skiing, backcountry treks & snowshoe outings
in and around Lake Superior's Sawtooth Mountains

Copyright © 1997 Andrew Slade
Maps © 1997 Sally Rauschenfels

Cover and book design: Sally Rauschenfels
Front cover photographs:
Gooseberry Falls State Park © Rudi Hargesheimer;
Skiers at Pincushion Mountain © Grand Marais Chamber of Commerce
Back cover photograph: © Minnesota Office of Tourism
Interior book photographs as noted: © Rudi Hargesheimer

A percentage of the royalties from the sale of this book will be donated to
organizations dedicated to the preservation, grooming and development of
cross-country ski trails along Minnesota's North Shore.

Although the author and publisher have researched all sources to ensure the
accuracy and completeness of the information contained in this book,
we assume no responsibility for errors, inaccuracies, omissions or any
inconsistency herein.

ISBN: 0-9636598-9-8

Library of Congress Cataloging in Publication Data
Slade, Andrew, 1964–
    White woods, quiet trails: exploring Minnesota's north shore in
winter / Andrew Slade.
    p.   cm.
    Includes index.
    ISBN 0-9636598-9-8
    1. Cross-country skiing—Minnesota—Sawtooth Mountains Region—
Guidebooks. 2. Hiking—Minnesota—Sawtooth Mountains Region—
Guidebooks. 3. Snowshoes and snowshoeing—Minnesota—Sawtooth
Mountains Region—Guidebooks. 4. Backpacking—Minnesota—Sawtooth
Mountains Region—Guidebooks. 5. Sawtooth Mountains Region (Minn.)—
Guidebooks.   I. Title.
GV854.5.S28S53   1997   97-30755
796.93'2'0977675—dc21   CIP

FIRST PRINTING October 1997

Ridgeline Press
PO Box 4, Two Harbors MN 55616-4004   Tel (218) 834-4436

This book is dedicated to our son, Hans Erich Slade,
who skied many of these trails in utero or in a backpack.
May he come to love the sound of popping birches,
the smell of a campfire and the feel of good ski wax.

Acknowledgements

This book would not have been possible without the tireless cooperation of the dozens of winter recreation lovers who groom the trails in winter, clear and build them in the summer and promote their use year-round. Special thanks to Kelly Fleissner, John Paulso, Gary Hoeft, Gary Nelson, the Lutsen-Tofte Tourism Association, Bill and Beth Blank, Dave Williams, Scott Beattie, Susan Kerfoot, Dan Baumann and Barb and Ted Young for their extra time and help.

The Superior Hiking Trail Association is taking the lead in promoting quiet sports on the North Shore. This book is an affirmation of their love and care for the region. The board of directors committed early to this project and have supported it throughout.

Rudi Hargesheimer's photographs give the book a beautiful reality. Special thanks to him for sharing his work both on this book and with the Superior Hiking Trail in general.

This book was truly a family effort. Without the babysitting of Alyce, Anita and Malina Rauschenfels, much of Sally's design work would never have been completed. Critical editing and proofreading was provided by Dick and Ella Slade, who carried manuscripts to England and Montana. Any typo in the book, especially the letters M,N or B, is likely the work of our one-year-old son Hans, who was always bapping the keyboard.

Sally Rauschenfels is the true genius of this book. It was her vision that created it and her motivation that has seen it through. I would have been lost without her.

Finally, a big thank you to Lake Superior. If it weren't for you, none of this would be here, including me.

—*Andrew Slade*

Contents

Foreword

The day was one of those blue-wax classics. Temperature somewhere in the 20s, a sky you could reach up and touch, sunshine bathing the Sawtooth Mountains on Minnesota's North Shore.

Four of us had made the climb on cross-country skis to Nipisiquit Lake in Tettegouche State Park. We continued to climb as the trail left the lake and finally topped the ridge.

I remember double-poling at the lip of the downhill run. This descent was new to all of us, who were skiing Tettegouche for the first time. None of us will forget it.

The downhill begins innocently enough, then begins to drop seriously. Soon, tears begin forming in the corners of your eyes, and you hear any loose clothing flapping madly. Still the drop goes on. The run carves its way around a just-manageable curve and keeps on dropping.

Now you're beginning to ache a little in your tuck, but you don't dare come out of it. You want nothing to blemish this marvelous run. To this day, I'm not sure how long that run is, but it must be one of the longest descents on the Shore.

We were giddy as, one by one, we coasted to a halt where the run leveled off. Giddy with the exhilaration of the run, the gift of the day, the good fortune of living on the North Shore.

Those beautiful trails at Tettegouche are just one of forty-one Andrew Slade describes in the following pages. With the same precision and accuracy he exercised in putting together his *Guide to the Superior Hiking Trail*, Slade concisely summarizes hundreds of kilometers of cross-country ski trails that snake through the woods from Duluth to the Canadian border in the Sawtooth Mountains.

From state parks to Snowflake Nordic Center, from Cascade Lodge to Korkki Nordic, they are all here. Although I've skied many of these systems, I was still astounded at just how much skiing we have along the Shore. Some of these systems have come only in the past few years, and some have been refined and upgraded significantly in the past decade or so. The time was right for a book like this.

Before turning you loose on these trails, Slade offers a short course in the wonders of snow, the adaptations of critters and the right trail clothing. He also addresses two growing forms of winter exploration—river skiing and snowshoeing.

It is perhaps just coincidence that this book has come off the press after two of the longest, snowiest and coldest winters in northern Minnesota's history. If you live in the North, you have two options every winter—endure it or embrace it. This book, both in spirit and in its wealth of information, is for those who embrace winter.

—*Sam Cook*
Duluth News-Tribune Outdoors Writer
Duluth, Minnesota

Author's welcome

You hold in your hand a key. My hope is that these pages will open the door to many wonderful winter experiences for you, your friends and family. Writing this book has been a joy for me, especially the "research" part. If I have done my job well, the headaches and confusion of finding and understanding new places to experience winter will be gone, and you will be enjoying all the magic which winter on the North Shore has to offer.

I'd ask you to imagine the first snowfall of the year. How do you feel? After a lush, fragrant summer and a quick, dramatic fall, those first white flakes slanting out of a gray November sky can be at once exciting and ominous, brilliant and somber. To a child, the first snowfall is an invitation to slide on the barest of snow-covered slopes on the thinnest of cardboard sleds. But to many adults, the return of a snowy landscape means driving to work on slippery roads. Winter can mean a thousand things to a thousand different people. We yield reluctantly our wooded path, our clear lawn, our dry streets. Shutting the storm windows and putting away the screens in anticipation of cold ahead must include some melancholy.

Hold off that melancholy. A lucky bit of geology a billion years ago left northern Minnesota with the rugged topography of the Sawtooth Mountains. Throw in the glaciers of the last ice age and you get the world's largest freshwater lake. Combine these two today and you get some of the best winter recreation in the Midwest. With abundant snowfall from moisture off Lake Superior and rugged ridgelines that sweep down to the shore, you get unbeatable cross-country skiing terrain. Add 100 years of hospitality and volunteer trail building from the descendents of loggers and fishing families, and you get a down-home, yet world-class, winter experience.

Whether you're skiing on a groomed trail through maples or bushwhacking on snowshoes through a spruce bog, if I have done my job well you'll find winter to be beautiful if not gorgeous, quiet if not serene, and exciting if not scary.

Here's what I recommend: lay face down on three feet of dark Lake Superior ice and be absorbed by the whale calls of shifting ice. Unpack and devour the most delicious lunch of bagels and cheese you ever tasted. If the days are too short, get out at night in a full moon and let the shadows fuel your imagination. Ski a lantern-lit trail, then take a sauna and plunge through a hole in the ice and holler "Uff da!" This winter land, its people and its creatures, will take root in your heart.

—*Andrew Slade*
Duluth, Minnesota

Ecology of the
North Shore
in Winter

Going out on the North Shore for a ski or snowshoe trek? Well, be sure to prepare yourself. Bring the right stuff, do the right things, and you'll be set. Surviving the winter woods is easy. And you can learn how other creatures of the North Shore survive as well.

When you go out for a ski around a loop or a trek up a frozen river, you will encounter the same conditions faced by the plants and animals that live there. And you *adapt* to the conditions, either by *doing* something or *having* something. Just as you put on layers of clothes to keep out the chill, just as you have something on your feet with more surface area than your own soles, all those plants and animals have or do things to adapt to winter as well.

In winter, the primary conditions to which all plants and animals must adapt are cold air, dry air and deep snow.

All organisms that you might encounter on your winter trek have successfully adapted to all of these conditions, in ways that range from the simple to the beautifully complex. Some adaptations are things that the organism *has,* such as the wide feet of a snowshoe hare. Some are things the organism *does,* such as the yarding of the white-tailed deer.

THE GEOGRAPHY OF WINTER

The North Shore represents the juncture between land and water—between the relatively rugged terrain of the ridgeline and the wild depths of the world's largest freshwater sea. In order to understand winter ecology of the area, you have to understand a little about the two "sides" of the North Shore.

While the shoreline itself is a wonderful place to explore, especially in winter, most of the trails and opportunities described in this book are inland from the shore itself, in the hills that parallel the shore. This is elevated terrain that stretches virtually uninterrupted from Superior, Wisconsin to Thunder Bay, Ontario and beyond, a ridgeline typically 600 to 1200 feet above the level of Lake Superior. It is known to ecologists as the "Superior Highlands" and to geologists and hopeful geographers as the "Sawtooth Mountains."

On the other "side" of the North Shore is Lake Superior, by surface area the largest freshwater lake in the world, holding 10% of the world's surface fresh water. The lake strongly influences the life around it by creating a unique microclimate near the shoreline. Within ten miles of Lake Superior, you will find a climate that is both warmer and snowier than the rest of the region. This leads to distinct changes in the flora and fauna, as well as some excellent winter recreation opportunities.

Warmer by the Lake. Lake Superior is a thermal flywheel. Its vast volume of water (estimated at 3 *quadrillion* gallons) is slow to change in response to seasonal change in temperature. The average temperature of the lake is 39°F, and this increases or decreases by only 8°F all year long. While the air temperature in this region is warmest in early August and coldest in mid-January, Lake Superior water is warmest in mid-September and coldest in March.

The net effect is that during the winter, the lake acts as a heater. While 35°F water seems bone-chilling to most, when the air temperature is −40°F in the region, that water is a noticeable source of warmth. Listen to an early morning January weather report; on a cold night statewide, Duluth (or better, Grand Marais) will often be the warmest spot in the state. It can be 20°F warmer at the shore of the lake than at a spot a few miles inland.

Lake-effect snow. Snow is a form of precipitation. Precipitation occurs when a mass of air loses the ability to hold on to some or all of the moisture it contains. This typically happens when the air mass is cooled, either by rising in elevation and cooling as the air mass expands, or when the air mass encounters something colder than itself, either another air mass or colder land.

Winter air masses, especially those that come out of northern Canada, are typically quite dry. When one of these dry winter air masses comes sliding across the vast, moist expanse of Lake Superior, it picks up a lot of moisture, forming clouds. When these clouds hit the cooler land, especially where there is some elevation change in the landscape (with every 1000-foot increase in elevation, the temperature cools 3°-5°F), they drop their moisture in the form of light, fluffy snow, known as "lake-effect snow."

From the Minnesota shore on a day when a cold northwest wind blows, you can see the wind literally "picking up steam." The dry air draws evaporation from the lake surface and carries it off in growing, billowing clouds to the Wisconsin and Michigan shores. Lucky them. Towns like Houghton, Michigan and Hurley, Wisconsin are renown for their average snowfalls exceeding 200 inches a year.

This sort of snow is not as common on the North Shore. In order for true lake-effect snow to hit the North Shore, there must be a cool air mass coming from the east, south or southeast. This is associated with a low pressure system passing to the south of Lake Superior. A North Shore lake-effect storm can bring up to five feet of snow in one incident.

IT'S "SNOW" WONDER

The ample snow that falls on the North Shore, especially on the ridgeline, is both boon and bane for the organisms that live there. All plants and animals that live along the North Shore are in some way adapted to the presence of snow in the winter. For many, the snow is to their advantage; others have figured out ways to make the best of a bad situation. For example:

Snow insulates. A thick blanket of snow provides an ideal environment for protection from both cold and predators. While the temperature of the snow itself is below the freezing point, it acts as an ideal insulator: light, thick, full of air pockets. This means that the deeper the snow, the warmer it is underneath it—up to a point. Under a foot or two of snow, the temperature at ground level, where the snow meets the soil, is often at 30°F, even when the air temperature is 0°F or below. In this relatively warm area, small mammals thrive, in a subnivean network of tunnels, safe both from cold and from the eyes of hungry owls or shrikes.

Snow changes the rules of travel. Snow also changes the rules of travel. Animals must either have some physical feature—like big feet—to help them stay above the snow, or they must change their behavior to make the best of the situation, like white-tailed deer do when they create their network of trails.

GREEN SKIN AND ANTIFREEZE: PLANT SURVIVAL TRICKS

How do plants deal with winter? As best they can. They do not have the ability to migrate, so they have evolved a variety of coping mechanisms, including antifreeze in their cells, green bark and a heavy reliance on rootstock.

Each microclimate along the shoreline has its own particular type of plant life. The result of these thermal and snowy effects is a relatively predictable profile of forest types. The ridgeline of the more gentle hills is often nearly pure sugar maple and yellow birch, trees adapted to the warmer climate provided by the proximity of Lake Superior. These hills shed cold into the valleys below, where you'll find trees more tolerant of cold, like spruce, alder and ash. These valley trees have limber branches that can bend under the weight of snow and not break. This change in forest type from ridge to valley is clear when you ski down from the ridgeline.

Buried alive: green plants under white snow. Snow also protects plants from the dryness of winter air. Dig under the snow in a marshy area and you might find green plants, like labrador tea or wintergreen, their evergreen leaves protected from the dry winter air by the moisture of the snow. Some other common evergreen plants include leatherleaf, polypody fern, twinflower, pyrola and pipsissewa.

Antifreeze and Chapstik®. The evergreen trees, like spruce and pine, use some remarkable tricks to survive winter's cold, dry air. Normally when a cell freezes it is killed. During the fall, before hard frosts arrive, the cells in the needles gradually lose water content. Less water means a higher percentage of the natural sugars found in the cells. Eventually the level of sugars inside the cell is high enough to act as an antifreeze.

At the same time, the outside of the needle develops a waxy coating. Try gently breaking off some needles and smelling them; there shouldn't be much smell. Then crush the needles with your fingers and smell again. Having broken the waxy, Chapstik®-like coating, you can now smell the strong scent of a conifer.

Kamikaze survival. What better way to live than to die? That's the ironic survival technique of many northwoods wildflowers and ferns, though you won't see much sign of this in winter. Since keeping a leafy plant alive through the winter presents so many challenges, it's far more energy-efficient for a plant to store up nutrients in the summer, die back to its roots in the fall, wait out the winter underground, and then send up new shoots in the spring. Most of the wildflowers in the North Woods survive in just this way. The other, less common option is to overwinter as a seed, protected under the snow and ready to sprout and grow in spring.

CLEVER ANIMAL TRICKS

In the depths of winter, when everything ought to be still and quiet, the forest seems to come alive. When traveling these woods in winter, the whole drama of wildlife activity becomes apparent even to the most casual observer. Animal tracks, including birds, tell stories of survival and challenge to rival anything Mutual of Omaha ever brought you.

Surprisingly, the overall caloric requirements of animals do not increase greatly in winter. While in summer animals spend time traveling to different feeding sites, seeking mates and other important tasks, in winter their activity level is relatively lower. Calories are burned largely in staying warm. Many mammals lose significant amounts of weight during the winter—up to one-third their body mass. This is the result of lowered calorie intake, but is also helpful for reducing overall calorie requirements; the lighter an animal is, the less energy is required to stay warm.

There are three general strategies animals use in winter along the North Shore:

Go to the Lake: local migration. Since in winter it is often warmer by Lake Superior, there is also less snow by the lake, as the warmth melts the snow. This provides an oasis for the animals of northeastern Minnesota. White-tailed deer come from twenty or thirty miles away in the winter to spend the coldest months near the lakeshore. They take advantage of the shallower snowpack, created by warmer days and sunshine on the south-facing slopes common to the shore area, leaving deep inland snows behind.

Fur finesse: coat changes. Most mammals undergo some sort of change in their fur for winter survival, either thickening, changing color or both. The advantage of thicker fur is obvious. But the reason for color change might not be what you think. The change from summer brown or grey to winter white by the short-tailed weasel and snowshoe hare is indeed an advantage for camouflage. But the white color also comes from the emptying of color pigment from otherwise hollow strands of fur; this added air space increases the insulation value of the fur.

All together now: group dynamics. Whether it's birds, deer or snakes, animals of one species or of different species tend to gather in winter to share warmth, feeding and trails. Deer mice cuddle in groups under the snow. Birds of different species, including chickadees, woodpeckers and nuthatches, collect in mixed flocks to forage for the limited food available. Deer, moose and wolves will travel on the same packed trail through the snow (albeit at different times). Ravens follow a wolf pack to its kills, or alert wolves to a carcass. As with humans, winter brings out the cooperative spirit in the animal kingdom.

For those animals unable to deal directly with winter, options include:

The deep sleep: hibernation and torpor. Many animals utilize some form of winter dormancy to survive until spring. For animals like the black bear that survive on soft, living things like berries and insects, there is no available winter food source. So after a summer and fall of eating everything in sight, they settle into a cave or under a fallen tree and their metabolism drops to a fraction of its winter rate. There are few true hibernators in the North Woods (the chipmunk is one); most winter-dormant animals (like the black bear) are inactive for shorter periods but wake partially for important events like giving birth. These shorter periods of dormancy are known as torpor.

The long good-bye: migration. Some animals, especially the birds, that we might think of as being distinctly North Woods or North Shore creatures, actually have another life somewhere else. When they can't survive the winter here and can't hibernate, animals of summer have to leave, and few are as able to travel long distance as birds. So the white-throated sparrow singing in the summer woods or the loon calling from the lake have adapted to our long winters simply by leaving.

ENVIRONMENTAL CONCERNS

In winter, the term "balance of nature" is particularly meaningful. The winter habitat stretches the capacity of organisms and ecosystems to their maximum. The line between survival and death is often narrow. Because of this fragile balance, winter presents some unique environmental issues of which the winter adventurer should be aware.

Human disturbance and animal energy balance. The energy balance of a given animal is tightly budgeted. Every time they have to move, energy is required. If you have a tight monthly budget and suddenly your roof starts leaking, you hope to have enough in reserve to fix the roof. For a deer, wolf or fox, there isn't always a reserve. That's why it's so important to avoid disturbing animals in winter. Every time a grouse gets scared up from its hole in the snow by a snowshoer, or a deer from its bed by a skier, it's spending energy it might not be able to spare. While it's fun to see these animals when we're out in the woods, keep your distance. Let them ramble off the ski trail rather than scaring them away.

Acid snow. For reasons that aren't yet clear, precipitation on the North Shore tends to be among the most acidic in the state of Minnesota. The climatological phenomena associated with land meeting shore seem to attract the particulate-laden rainfall from sources hundreds of miles away. Whereas in the summer this is known as "acid rain," in the winter it is "acid snow." During spring, this acid snow melts and brings a pulse of acidity down the North Shore streams, as six months of acid precipitation is released all at once. This remote and beautiful area does suffer under the influence of distant pollution sources.

Get out and enjoy, and let the stories of life and beautiful survival unfold as you ski or snowshoe through these woods.

Winter
Safety
Basics

Winter transforms the land. A dense green forest becomes a bright white landscape. With the change in scenery comes a change in the environment—a new set of both opportunities and concerns.

Winter is not forgiving of mistakes. Fortunately we have on the North Shore a well-developed network of winter recreation opportunities, so that the avid newcomer to winter can venture out with relative safety. Cross-country skiing on the Sugarbush trails is not exactly like heading for the North Pole. Yet some of the same concerns do exist.

CONCERNS OF WINTER

Primary winter factors. Just as plants and animals have to adapt to winter, so must humans. And the primary factors to which we must adjust are the same:

- **Cold air.** The difference between our body temperature and the outside temperature can be as much as 140°F. The greater the difference, the faster we lose heat.

- **Dry air.** Because winter air is cold, it cannot hold as much moisture. Plus, we live far from a source of moisture like an ocean. So winter air is very dry. The steam you exhale on a winter day is a sign of this.

- **Deep snow.** Travel in winter takes on whole new challenges.

As you consider winter safety, factors that are less important for plants and animals become more important for humans:

- **Wet air.** Moisture in the air, although limited in winter, increases its ability to chill. Also, in early and late winter, occasional rainfall can trouble the unprepared adventurer.

- **Wind.** The wind chill factor becomes more than just a number on the radio when you're out on an exposed ridge and the air temperature is 0°F.

- **Sun.** While the sun is an asset for staying warm, sunshine can be hazardous to exposed skin and eyes.

Staying safe and warm in the winter is a matter of proper preparation, proper equipment and safe behavior in the field.

WHAT TO BRING

Proper equipment for winter travel is *not* a matter of the most expensive labels or highest technology.

Clothing. Your winter adventure wardrobe should rely heavily on those fabrics which will keep you warm even if they get wet, and on clothing that will keep you from getting wet in the first place. In winter, wetness comes more often from inside—from your own perspiration. But in certain conditions it can also come from outside.

When clothes get wet, they lose their ability to keep you warm. The sweat you make when you're hot and exercising will dampen your clothes and make you cold soon.

The best technique is to avoid perspiring in the first place. This means dressing in layers and, sometimes, wearing surprisingly few clothes even when it's quite cold. On a 10°F day, an active cross-country skier or snowshoer can be quite comfortable in long underwear and a windbreaker, gloves and a headband. Of course, as soon as they stop moving, they'll want another layer or two, a hat and mittens.

Use the following guidelines to select your clothes for a winter outing:

- **Underwear layer.** Next to your skin, both on top and on bottom, should be a fabric that can wick moisture away from your skin, dry

Great snacks to take in your fanny pack

Q. What's compact, hard to break, unfreezeable and full of complex carbos?

A. The ideal trail snack, that's what!

For outings longer than an hour, pack away some extra fuel like raisins, peanuts or their yogurt-covered cousins. Hard cheeses hold up well, but slice them before you head out. Lots of people like oranges because they taste great outdoors and add liquid, too; they can be a hassle for cold fingers, so try peeling them ahead of time. Don't bother with anything wrapped up like chocolate candies; you'll be a litterbug for sure. ✸

quickly and be warm when wet. This is most often a synthetic fabric like polypropylene, known under different brand names such as Thermax® or Capilene®. A lightweight synthetic pile like Polartec® can also serve as a first layer. Wool (and silk to a lesser degree) are natural fibers that can also wick moisture and keep you warm when wet. Cotton long johns and turtlenecks, while comfortable, will absorb your perspiration and chill you, so should be used only on very short outings (under an hour) with caution.

• **Insulation layer.** The key to insulation is trapped air. Pockets of dead air space absorb heat and act as a buffer between your warm skin and the cold outside. This layer should be made of either thick, warm-when-wet material such as polyester fleece, Thinsulate® or wool, or of a puffy material, such as down or a synthetic fill like Polargard® or Quallofil®. But don't choose a too-thick jacket—the Michelin-man look is too warm for real layering.

• **Protective layer.** Also known as the "environmental layer," this is the outer shell that keeps wind, wet snow and rain from penetrating to you and your other layers. This layer should be "breathable"—it should allow moisture from your body to escape while still keeping the elements (wind and water) out. Fabrics such as Gore-Tex® provide this sort of protection, but during most of the winter all you need is a light nylon windbreaker. Only in late fall or early spring, when rain is a real possibility, should you worry much about water re-

---

Equipment list for <u>short</u> outings (0–8K skiing, 1–2 hours snowshoeing)

• top: underwear layer, insulation layer, protective layer

• bottom: underwear layer, protective layer (or one that combines both)

• hat *or* headband

• gloves

• footwear: liner socks (silk or polypropylene), heavy socks (wool or synthetic), boots (ski boots for skiing, insulated boots with liners or mukluks for snowshoeing)

• sunglasses

• sunscreen

• gaiters, if skiing in fresh snow or snowshoeing

• wax equipment, if necessary: a range of waxes on both sides of today's current wax, wax scraper and cork

• water (one quart for two people)

• cross-country ski license

• energy food

Whatever you don't wear will probably fit into a fanny pack. ❄

sistance. Typically a rain jacket sacrifices too much in breathability in winter, and you'll end up with frost crystals inside your jacket. If you are snowshoeing or enjoying other activities where a "close encounter" with snow is likely, a layer that is more waterproof is appropriate, especially on your lower body.

- **Extremities.** Layering also works for your head, hands and feet. In the case of your head, either a headband, earmuffs or a hat will work, depending on the temperature. Taking off your hat is a great way to regulate your temperature if you're getting too warm, but increases the risk of frostbite on your earlobes. A neck gaiter is great both for your neck and for your chin and nose. Mittens generally keep your hands warmer than gloves. With your feet, dress in layers both for warmth and for blister protection—a thin pair of liner socks can work wonders for the blister prone.

When you are active on the trail, often just the underwear layer and the protective layer will be enough. But as soon as you stop, you'll want to pull on the insulation layer as well.

STAYING FOUND

If you are simply staying on groomed ski trails or on a single river, getting lost should not be a problem. Most ski trails are quite well marked, with "you are here" maps at most or all intersections. On trips of an hour or less, you shouldn't even need to have a map with you (but photocopy the one from this book anyway to be on the safe side).

Navigation. The best way to figure out where you are is to know where you are all along. Make predictions and watch them come true. If the map says that the next intersection should be the Pine Hills Trail on the left, watch and be sure it is.

When snowshoeing on the Superior Hiking Trail or other non-groomed, irregularly marked trails, navigation becomes much more important. Even the most experienced snowshoers get lost on the

Superior Hiking Trail. For more information, see the chapter "Snowshoeing the North Shore's Winter Woods."

Be known. If you're going to be out for more than a few hours, be sure someone knows where you are going and when to expect you back. Let them know what they should do if you don't come back on time. Options would include contacting local authorities or staff at trailhead facilities. In the highly unusual case that you're not back on time, but stuck in the woods hoping for help, thinking and planning ahead like this could save your life.

STAYING WARM

It sounds silly, but the best way to avoid getting cold is not to get hot. Overheating means sweat, which means moisture in your clothes, which means getting chilled as soon as you stop. Dressing in layers and knowing when to take off a layer will keep you feeling "just right."

Hypothermia is the lowering of core body temperature below normal levels. It sneaks up on its victims. It is caused most often by gradual chilling, often in connection with moisture.

Moisture can come from rain as well as sweat. It's no surprise that the greatest number of cases of hypothermia come not in the middle of winter but in the late fall and early spring when it's around 40°F and raining. Hypothermia typically comes on slowly and is generally a problem only when people are out for a long time or someone suddenly gets wet. In the middle of winter, this can happen from falling through the ice of a lake or river; if this happens, the person must change clothes immediately.

Equipment list for day-long outings (8K–30K skiing, 2–8 hours snowshoeing). Add to list for short outing:

- extra water: one to two quarts per person, insulated

- more food: high-energy bag lunch, candy bar, orange slices

- hat *and* headband

- extra insulation layer, especially if traveling over water

- extra socks

- area map

- matches

- first aid kit

- flashlight (optional)

- ski or snowshoe repair kit: tape, replacement ski tip (optional)

This will probably require a small or medium-sized day pack.

It's important to remember that it's not enough just to bring the right stuff. You have to know when and how to use it. ❅

The other major reason for getting cold in winter is the wind and the wind chill factor. When the wind is blowing, don't take your breaks on exposed ridges, but rather stay down in the wooded valleys out of the wind. Be sure not to ski too far with a tail wind if you have to turn around and ski back into the wind.

Avoiding frostbite. When the temperature gets below freezing, frostbite becomes more of a danger than hypothermia. Exposed skin can literally freeze, causing minor to major damage to the tissue of ears, nose and cheeks. Covered extremities like fingers or toes can also freeze, although this takes longer to occur. When the air temperature or wind chill drops below about 10°F, frostbite becomes a real issue. Keep your extremities covered and keep good circulation in your feet and hands. Too-tight ski boots restrict the flow of blood to your toes and increase the risk of frostbite. As part of your breaks for water or snacks, twinkle your toes and drum your fingers to keep the blood flowing.

STAYING HEALTHY

Avoiding sun exposure. Just because the sun is low in winter doesn't mean it can't do any harm. Especially in spring, sunburn and snowblindness become real concerns. Bring sunscreen, lip balm and sunglasses. Even on a cloudy day the brightness can be harmful. As a general rule of thumb, if you're squinting you should have on sunglasses, and if you have sunglasses on in the middle of the day you should have sunscreen on as well.

Avoiding dehydration. When active outdoors, your body requires around four quarts of water a day. So when you're out for more than an hour or so, bring plenty of liquids and keep drinking them. Fill one bottle with warm or hot water and cover it with a sock or other insulation; by the end of the day, it will be cooled off but not frozen. Don't eat snow for liquid; the energy required to melt it requires more water than you gain.

Staying safe in winter is a matter of careful and conservative planning, active care for your bodily needs and respect for the winter environment. The magic of winter in the deep forest is well worth the effort.

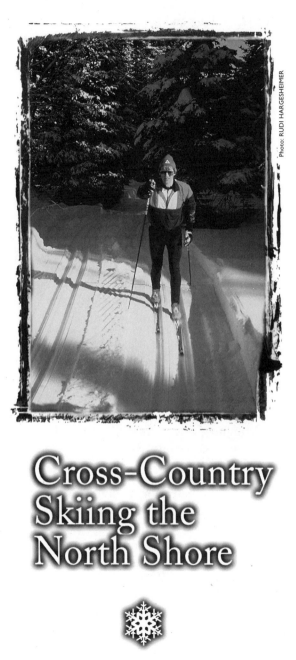

Cross-Country Skiing the North Shore

❄

Jackrabbit Johannsen. Snowshoe Thompson. Fridtjof Nansen. Heming the Viking and his magic skis. The history of cross-country skiing is long and mostly Scandinavian. What began 4000 years ago in Norway and flourished in the snowy Nordic countries has become global in its appeal. In seventh-century China snowbound hunters used "wooden horses" on their feet and "props" under their arms. According to descriptions of the time, "they went forward at least one hundred paces with every stride."

Cross-country skiing came to America with Scandinavian immigrants. Jackrabbit Johannsen, a Canadian engineer, was an early promoter of the sport. In the California Gold Rush years, Scandinavian fortune seekers like Norwegian Snowshoe Thompson used their handmade skis to deliver mail and play on the snowy mountains.

Skiing in northern Minnesota. The first ski club in Minnesota was organized in the early 1880s. But these early pioneers could hardly sustain their hobby through two world wars and the rush for cars and fast toys that followed them.

Through the postwar years, skiing was the hobby of a dedicated few. Korkki Nordic in rural Duluth was an early center of skiing, with trails built by Charlie Banks in 1954 and still used today by advocates of traditional diagonal skiing. In the mid-1960s, state high-school skiing championships were held on a Duluth course that combined the current Chester Bowl trails, crossed Kenwood Avenue and continued in the woods behind the College of St. Scholastica.

In the late 1960s, cross-country skiing was reborn. The North Star Ski Touring Club was established in 1967, from a local committee of the United States Ski Association. Ski advocates had to fight for the political recognition necessary for successful building and maintenance of trails. Grant-in-aid money from state gas revenues went to local clubs and agencies to develop trails. Trails in Jay Cooke State Park were part of an early push by Minnesota State Parks to enhance skiing opportunities.

A 1977 effort by Governor Rudy Perpich to make Minnesota the "Ski Touring Capital of the Nation" resulted in a flurry of ac-

tivity with new standards, legislation and trail signage. But much more than the work of government funds, individual volunteers were responsible for most of the trails we see today. Foresighted local skiers and resort owners, with training from state and national clubs, made up crews that built hundreds, even thousands, of miles of ski trails. Between 1978 and 1983, total numbers of skiers in the state doubled from 500,000 to over 1,000,000. In 1983, northeastern Minnesota had 742 miles of ski trail. This included the North Shore Mountains system, which was first to break the mold of unconnected local ski areas by connecting many smaller local areas into one large system, in cooperation with local tourism facilities.

Despite the hard work of volunteers, however, some money was always necessary to fuel the chainsaws and pay for the grooming equipment. In 1982, the small amount of grant money for ski trails from unrefunded gasoline taxes was taken away. In response, a statewide ski trail permit fee was created in 1983 and has existed largely unchanged since then.

Evolution of technique and equipment. Recent developments in technology and technique have taken the traditional image of a skier (imagine a full-blooded Norwegian gliding along a narrow trail on long wooden skis with a combination of tar and suet on the base, wearing wool knickers,

Fun with ski wax

Avid skiers talk ski wax like baseball fans discuss hitting statistics. Here's a sample quote: "Well, it's in the 30s and I thought it was a klister day but I gobbed some yellow in the kick zone and I got some good grab." For extra, equally comprehensible fun, try reading aloud the Norwegian and Finnish instructions on the stubs of your leftover wax. But seriously, good waxing is a wonderful addition to your ski day, and bad waxing can be a serious detriment. Here are some tips:

• When in doubt, err on the "cold" side, especially in fresh snow. It's better to not stick than to stick too much.

• If you are slipping too much, the answer might be in your hands: try putting more weight on your poles.

• If that doesn't work, just apply some "TLC." "T" is for "thicker," i.e. apply your existing wax thicker. If that doesn't work, try "L" for "longer," filling in more of your kick zone with wax. Finally, you can try "C" for "change"— change to the next warmer wax. ❄

checkered socks and a funny hat, with a water pouch slung around the neck) and made it a quaint symbol. Today's skier is more likely to be using short, high-tech skis on a wide, double-tracked trail groomed that morning by a $50,000 Pisten-Bully groomer. The skier is likely to be wearing skintight Lycra and science fiction sunglasses, in colors normally seen in the woods only in the most exotic spring wildflower.

In the last twenty years, regular machine grooming of ski trails has come to be considered virtually mandatory for skiing enjoyment. There are still those who prefer the quiet and solitude of breaking their own trail, and plenty of these opportunities still exist. But overall, skiing on the North Shore has come to be associated with the technology of wider trail construction, machine grooming and excellent maps and signage.

The growth of machine grooming has encouraged new equipment and new techniques. Skis have gotten narrower and shorter; skis on a groomed trail don't require as much surface area to stay "afloat." Also, the technique of skate skiing, which requires wide, groomed trails, has become increasingly popular statewide. Many trails in this region are not suitable for skate skiing, so if you are a skate skier, choose your trail wisely to avoid disappointment.

EQUIPMENT

The equipment necessary for cross-country skiing makes it one of the more low-tech sports around. There are no motors or gears involved; high technology is something like a spring in a pole handle or a new mix of fibers for the ski. If you buy equipment, you should be able to get an adequate setup of skis, boots, bindings and poles for less than $200.

What sort of ski? Wax or no-wax? Get a grip! The middle of your skis have to grip the snow somehow. This comes down to a choice between waxable and no-wax skis.

No-wax skis are far easier to use than waxable skis. No-wax skis have a set of "fish scales" or other gripping surface in the area of the ski base under the boot. Most novices and many intermediates prefer no-wax skis. You can put them on and ski away. Their primary disadvantages are the noise they make and the fact that the fish scales slow you down significantly as they rub the snow.

Waxable skis are more of a hassle but are also faster, quieter and smoother. You have to choose (and sometime guess) which wax is good for the day, then spend five minutes or more scraping and rubbing at the bottom of your skis before you can hit the trail. The result is either a heavenly glide and terrific grip on the hills, or another five minutes of scraping and rubbing. There are also snow conditions, especially during and after a thaw, when almost no sane wax will work well (leaving klister to the not-so-sane).

Some have worked out a balance. Ski on waxable skis for the bulk of the year when there is fresh snow and temperatures under freezing. Get a used pair of no-wax skis for marginal conditions. Apply your time and energy appropriately.

GETTING EQUIPPED ON THE SHORE

So here you are, in cross-country ski heaven, and you don't have any skis? Either go to a full-service ski center and rent and ski there (see "Ski Centers" listing on page 22), or visit one of the following places, which rent or sell skis:

Duluth
- Continental Ski Shop, 1305 E. First Street (218) 728-4466
- North Star Bike and Boards, 4521 E. Superior Street (218) 525-7257
- Ski Hut, 1032 E. Fourth Street (218) 724-8525
- Play It Again Sport (used equipment), Kenwood Shopping Center (218) 724-1700

Superior
- Northwest Outlet, 1814 Belknap (715) 392-9838
- Superior Sports, 1210 Tower Avenue (715) 394-5600

Two Harbors area
- Avalanche Cycle, 602 1st Avenue, Two Harbors (218) 834-0555
- Cliff House Cabins and Bottle Shop, just east of Silver Cliff tunnel (218) 834-2030

Lutsen-Tofte area
- Sawbill Canoe Outfitters, Tofte (218) 387-1360
- Lutsen Resort, Lutsen (218) 663-7244

Grand Marais
- Bear Track Outfitting (218) 387-1162
- Wilderness Waters Outfitters (218) 387-2525

NORTH SHORE SKI CENTERS

The following North Shore facilities offer complete amenities for skiers, including on-site rentals, pass purchase and changing or warming rooms. All are located directly at trailheads. Many also offer professional ski instruction, ski repair and sales, refreshments and other goodies. For more information, see the individual trail descriptions.

- Spirit Mountain
- Snowflake Nordic Center
- Lutsen Mountains Nordic Center
- Solbakken
- Cascade Lodge
- Central Gunflint
- Upper Gunflint

PAYING YOUR DUES

There is almost no such thing as a free ski. If you find a trail that seems to be free, chances are there is an opportunity for you to help out either financially or physically. The North Shore is blessed with a tremendous wealth of skiing opportunities, built on all skiers pitching in and helping out.

Minnesota state passes. The Great Minnesota Ski Pass is an incredible bargain. Passes are required at twenty-seven of the thirty-seven Minnesota areas described in this book. The pass generates funds for building, maintaining and grooming Minnesota ski trails. Passes are available on a daily basis, a yearly basis, or for three years, and are available for both individuals and married couples. As of 1996-97, the pass costs:

Individual day	$1.00
Individual season	$5.00
Husband/Wife season	$7.50
Individual 3-year	$14.00
Husband/Wife 3-year	$21.00

The Great Minnesota Ski Pass is available by calling (800) 766-6000 or (612) 296-6157. It is also sold at state parks, county auditors and businesses such as ski shops. The pass really is required. If you are caught without a pass, the penalty is $70. Bring the pass with you when you ski: if you accidentally leave it at home there could still be a penalty.

Private areas. There are a number of cross-country ski areas in the region that are privately owned and maintained. These areas charge their own usage fees, typically $5 to $12 a day. Often these trail fees are included in the cost of lodging for guests at the nearby resorts. Annual and family passes are often available. The Great Minnesota Ski Pass is generally not required at these private areas, but inquire locally to be sure.

For the extra cost, skiers will find consistently well-groomed trails, generally excellent facilities and a nice variety of skiing challenges. For the total skiing vacation, these facilities are an excellent choice.

Local clubs. The tradition of volunteering and local involvement has not been lost in the growth of private resorts and the statewide pass. In fact, anywhere you ski there is likely a local group working hard year around to keep your skiing experience excellent. These groups survive on tiny annual budgets supported mostly by membership contributions. Addresses of local clubs are included in the "Resources" chapter (page 173) of this book.

Since the statewide pass is such a good deal, take the time and the extra ten bucks or so to join and support one of these local clubs as well. Your money will be well spent. A little sweat equity always helps as well; volunteer hours in the fall clearing trails, in the winter filling bare spots and in the spring cleaning debris.

Wisconsin and Ontario. For those areas in this book outside of Minnesota, check the individual listing for pass requirements.

RULES OF THE ROAD

Regardless of where you ski, some basic rules of courtesy and safety apply.

Follow designated trail directions. This is for your safety and your enjoyment. One-way trails keep skiers from running into each other on hills and blind turns. They also keep skiing parties separate from each other, giving more of a wilderness feel to the experience.

Dogs are not allowed on trails. With very few exceptions, dogs should not be taken on your ski outing. They scare away wildlife and mess up the groomed trail with their feet and their feces.

Fill in "sitzmarks" if you fall. That crater of snow left from your spill will easily lead to another fall for the next skier. Pack in the snow again, run your skis through the groomed track and make it safe again.

Ski under control. If that hill seems too steep for you, snowplow or sidestep down. It is even okay to take off your skis and walk. This is both for your safety and the safety of the people below.

Do not obstruct the trail. When you take a break, step out of the track so that others can ski by. This is especially important if you are on a hill.

When removing skis and walking, walk on the side of the trail. Try to keep the groomed trail as neat as possible for the next skiers. In general, ski trails should not be used for either snowshoeing or hiking in winter.

A WORD ON TRAIL RATINGS

The difficulty ratings used in this book for trail descriptions and in trail maps are taken from the original, locally produced trail maps. There is no standard rating system for ski areas, either in the names of the levels or in what they mean. In general, however, use the guidelines below. Where the ratings seem truly inaccurate, the text makes that point.

Some trails are labelled "Easy," "Easier," "Beginner" or marked in the field with green circles. These are suitable for all skiers. The terrain is level; if there are uphills, skiers won't have to "herringbone," and any downhill will be easy with no turns and a long run-out.

Some trails are labelled "More Difficult," "Intermediate" or marked in the field with a blue square. These trails have some hills. Short uphills require a herringbone climb, and downhills require some ability to turn.

Some trails are labelled "Advanced," "Expert," "Most Difficult" or marked in the field with a black diamond. These require advanced skills such as snowplow turns and extended herringbone climbing. Expect sharp and steep turns on downhills (including hairpin turns) and long climbs.

ANDREW'S LISTS

The following lists are the author's somewhat arbitrary picks for top ski trails on the North Shore...all depending on what you are looking for. If your favorite isn't here, rest easy because absolutely no scientific procedure was applied.

Best grooming. Here are your best chances for smooth, fresh and neat grooming regardless of the conditions.

- Superior Municipal Forest
- Spirit Mountain
- Snowflake Nordic Center
- Korkki Nordic Ski Center
- Gooseberry Falls State Park
- Sugarbush
- Solbakken
- Cascade Lodge
- Pincushion Mountain
- Central Gunflint
- Upper Gunflint

Trails my mother would like. Gentle loops, not crowded, with a few easy hills and nice scenery.

- Jay Cooke State Park: CCC Trail
- Superior Municipal Forest: Red Loop
- Boulder Lake: Otter Run, Blue Ox
- Northwoods Ski Touring Trail: Inner Loops
- Flathorn-Gegoka: Central Loops
- Sugarbush: Wood Duck, Piece of Cake loops
- Moose Fence: Maple Loop
- Cascade River State Park: Cedar Woods
- George Washington Trail
- Central Gunflint: Summer Home Road, Ox Cart Trail
- Upper Gunflint: Big Pine Loop

Most likely to see wolf sign. Remote trails through wolf (and deer) habitat.

- Boulder Lake
- Korkki Nordic Ski Center
- Gooseberry Falls State Park
- Tettegouche State Park
- Flathorn-Gegoka
- Solbakken
- Cascade River State Park

Free. Trails with no permits or membership required.

- Boulder Lake
- George Washington Trail
- Rock Hill/Bagley Nature Area

Most remote feeling. Trails on which you can really get away from it all.

- Jay Cooke State Park: Spruce, High trails
- Magney-Snively
- Northwoods Ski Touring Trail: Tettegouche Connector
- Tettegouche State Park
- Sugarbush: Picnic Loop, Six-mile Crossing

- Banadad Trail
- Grand Portage

Longest season. Deep snow, some distance from Lake Superior, and quality, committed grooming.

- Snowflake Nordic Center
- Finland Ski Trail
- Flathorn-Gegoka
- Moose Fence
- Bear Track
- Pincushion Mountain
- Grand Portage

Best views of Lake Superior. From high bluffs or shoreline.

- Piedmont
- Chester Park
- Gooseberry Falls State Park
- Split Rock Lighthouse State Park
- Cascade River State Park: Lakeshore Loop, Moose Mountain
- Pincushion Mountain
- Judge C.R. Magney State Park

Downhill routes. Arrange a car shuttle so you can do these "norpine" trails from ridgeline to lakeshore.

- From Sawbill Trail to Tofte on Carlton Peak trails
- Lutsen Mountain Nordic Center (with chairlift)
- Caribou Trail to Solbakken
- Deer Yard to Cascade Lodge
- Bear Track to Cascade River State Park

Ski-through routes. Day-long journeys or longer for those who like to get from Point A to Point B or Z.

- Northwoods Ski Touring Trail to Tettegouche State Park trailhead
- Moose Fence to Oberg/Leveaux Mountains via Six-mile Crossing
- Lutsen Area to Solbakken

- Solbakken to Cascade Lodge
- Banadad Trail

Camping out. Bring your winter camping gear and head out to these remote campsites.

- Jay Cooke State Park
- Pattison State Park
- Boulder Lake (on ungroomed Wolf Bay Trail)
- Deer Yard (on Deer Yard Lake)
- Banadad Trail

Family friendly. Combination of easiest and advanced trails, plus warming hut and bathrooms.

- Jay Cooke State Park
- Superior Municipal Forest
- Spirit Mountain
- Snowflake Nordic Center
- Korkki Nordic Ski Center
- Split Rock Lighthouse State Park
- Central Gunflint
- Upper Gunflint

Best skate skiing. Wide, well-groomed trails where skate skiers won't have to worry about the diagonal track too much.

- Spirit Mountain
- Superior Municipal Forest
- Snowflake Nordic Center
- Lester Park
- Two Harbors Municipal Trail
- Moose Fence
- Oberg/Leveaux Mountains: Onion River Road
- Pincushion Mountain
- Central Gunflint: Old Logging Camp, Summer Home Road
- Upper Gunflint: West End Trail, Highland Trail

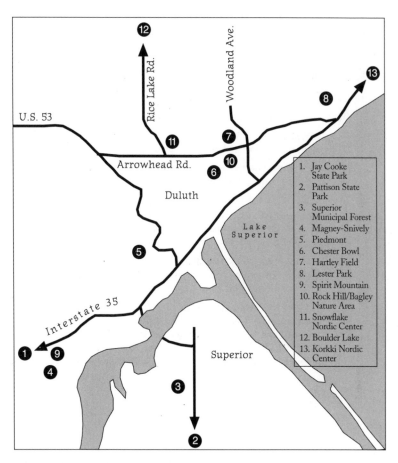

Map legend:

1. Jay Cooke State Park
2. Pattison State Park
3. Superior Municipal Forest
4. Magney-Snively
5. Piedmont
6. Chester Bowl
7. Hartley Field
8. Lester Park
9. Spirit Mountain
10. Rock Hill/Bagley Nature Area
11. Snowflake Nordic Center
12. Boulder Lake
13. Korkki Nordic Center

Map labels: U.S. 53, Rice Lake Rd., Woodland Ave., Arrowhead Rd., Duluth, Lake Superior, Interstate 35, Superior

Duluth-Superior Cross-Country Ski Trails

Blessed are the city dwellers! From anywhere within the city limits of Duluth and Superior, you are never more than a few miles away from some terrific skiing. From the wild curves and vast views of little Chester Bowl to the backcountry pines of Boulder Lake, from winter camping at Pattison State Park to the races at Snowflake Nordic Center, the range of options will keep any skier busy winter-long. While some of these trails are definitely urban, rolling through ballfields and backyards, others take you into wolf country and to unmatched scenic overlooks. Whether you're visiting or living here, you are in for some terrific, and varied, skiing.

Jay Cooke State Park

TRAILHEAD ACCESS
Drive three miles east of Carlton and Thomson on Highway 210.
Or drive from West Duluth and Fond du Lac west on Highway
210. The Oldenburg Point trailhead is approximately one mile
east of the main trailhead at the park office.

TOTAL TRAIL: 51K
Groomed Diagonal: 51K   Skating: 13.6K   Lit: none

PASS REQUIREMENTS
• Great Minnesota Ski Pass
• Minnesota State Park vehicle permit

TRAILHEAD FACILITIES
Chalet with bathrooms, vending machines, fireplace. Both ski
passes and vehicle permits are sold in the park office.

WHAT MAKES IT UNIQUE
Amazing amount of good skiing within easy access of Duluth.
Ski across a swinging bridge over the rugged St. Louis River.

INTERPRETIVE FEATURE
This landscape is both old and new. The sharp rocks in the wide
river bed are 1.6 billion year old metamorphic rocks like slate
and graywacke. However, much of the skiing is on red clay hills,
deposited 10,000 years ago under Glacial Lake Duluth.

South of Swinging Bridge

RIDGE TRAILS (4.5K)

EASIER / DIAGONAL ONLY

The only tough part about skiing these trails is getting across the
bridge and up the first hill. Fortunately for the beginning skier, a
lot of people walk this section—so you can walk this section and
not worry about trashing the trails. As the name implies, the Ridge
Trails traverse a ridge above the St. Louis River; the ridge is thick
with maples. With three smaller loops, this section is perfect for
goofing around with young kids.

SILVER CREEK AND BEAR CHASE TRAILS (10K)

INTERMEDIATE AND ADVANCED / DIAGONAL ONLY

These trails begin to take you into the backcountry of the park.
From here on out, the farther you go, the fewer people you will
see. The Silver Creek Trail is a 4.9K loop along the edge of the
river valley with great views, returning along Silver Creek's wet-

lands back to the Ridge Trails. As long as you've come this far, take the Bear Chase Trails too; the 5.1K of runs take you either through tight valleys or over narrow ridges for a fun, advanced ride.

UPPER AND LOWER LAKE TRAILS (5.8K)
ADVANCED / DIAGONAL ONLY
Lost Lake. The name gives this area a sense of adventure. These advanced trails will keep you huffing and puffing as you climb from the banks of the St. Louis River 200 feet up and glide back down again. These and the following trails are not groomed as often as the inner trails, so you might check with the park ranger before heading out here for the day.

SPRUCE AND HIGH TRAILS (8.8K)
INTERMEDIATE / DIAGONAL ONLY
Once past the advanced Lost Lake trails you enter more level, intermediate country which you're almost guaranteed to have to yourself. The Spruce Trail itself is a 6.8K loop; if that's not enough, take the High Trail 2K to an overlook of the St. Louis River (actually a reservoir here). It's over 11K from the swinging bridge to this overlook, so save energy for the way back.

North of Swinging Bridge

The trails north of the bridge start from the parking lot on the opposite side of the park office. Most skiers walk the thirty yards to the road and cross it before putting on their skis.

CCC TRAIL (3.4K)
EASIER / DIAGONAL ONLY
This trail takes old roadways through relatively open terrain around the campground. The eastern half in particular is very easy going after the first climb. The western half gets trickier when the trail leaves the old roadway and winds down to cross Highway 210. The return along the river bank is scenic any time of year.

WHITE PINE TRAIL (3.2K)
INTERMEDIATE / DIAGONAL AND SKATING
This is a delightful loop through dense groves of white pine and an open maple ridgeline. The first 0.4K follows an old roadbed downhill; the trail turns left off the old road and starts climbing

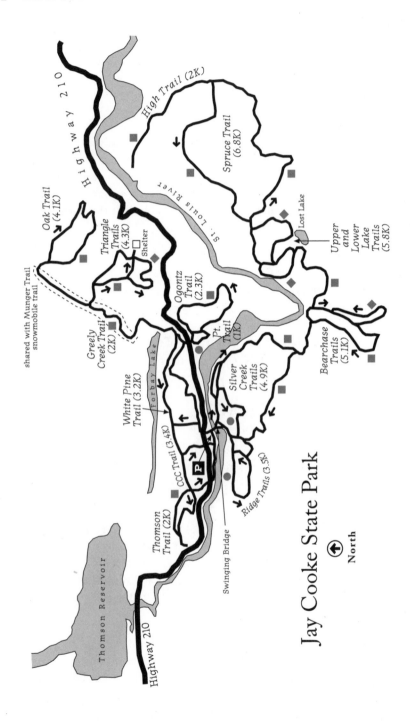

Highway 210

High Trail (2K.)

Spruce Trail (6.8K)

St. Louis River

Oak Trail (4.1K)

Lost Lake

Upper and Lower Lake Trails (5.8K)

Triangle Trails (4.3K)

Shelter

shared with Munger Trail snowmobile trail

Ogontz Trail (2.3K)

Greely Creek Trail (2K)

Pt. Trail (1K)

Bearchase Trails (5.1K)

White Pine Trail (3.2K)

Forbay Lake

Silver Creek Trails (4.9K)

CCC Trail (3.4K)

P

Ridge Trails (3.5K)

Thomson Trail (2K)

Swinging Bridge

Jay Cooke State Park

North

Thomson Reservoir

Highway 210

for a long herringbone up and around to a shelter with a great view of the St. Louis River valley. Enjoy a snack here as you take off for a day's ski. The trail winds through some rolling terrain on the south side, then levels out on the north side. Some of the turns are tricky here, so be prepared for quick moves.

THOMSON TRAIL (2K)
INTERMEDIATE / DIAGONAL ONLY

This is made "intermediate" by a daring swoop down and up past some large white pine. Otherwise this is mostly level terrain through open deciduous woods. History buffs can take the ungroomed 0.4K side trail to a 19th century cemetery.

OGANTZ AND POINT TRAILS (3.2K)
EASY AND INTERMEDIATE / DIAGONAL ONLY

Start your ski day at the Oldenburg Point picnic area and enjoy this exhilarating run through scenic territory. The Point Trail is an easy, almost 1K loop through the flats of the picnic area and includes the dramatic view from Oldenburg Point. The Ogantz Trail veers off the Point Trail and starts with a dramatic downhill run through an open oak forest. It then levels off and follows an old roadbed with some big willow trees alongside, before rolling very gradually back up to the parking lot through small openings and mixed forest.

Chickadees

The black-capped chickadee has a "bundle" of survival tricks, including bundling. Chickadees will, on cold nights, bundle together in a flock of around six birds in the hole of an evergreen tree and keep each other warm through the night. Chickadees can also go into a sort of torpor, letting their body temperatures drop by up to 12 degrees Celsius. They stay at this temperature through outbreaks of shivering. ❄

GREELY CREEK TRAIL (2K)
INTERMEDIATE / DIAGONAL AND SKATING

This trail connects the Oldenburg Point trails and the White Pine trails with the Triangle and Oak loops. The trail gives you a close-up look at the Thomson hydropower operations of Minnesota

Power, as it follows powerlines and then skirts the shore of Forbay Lake before crossing over the top of the small dam. Soon after the dam the trail joins the Willard Munger Trail, where you may briefly share the trail with snowmobiles.

TRIANGLE TRAILS (4.3K)
INTERMEDIATE TO ADVANCED / DIAGONAL AND SKATING
Pending access, this trail should be available to the public. There's a 2.2K intermediate loop with a spur to a shelter, plus a 1.3K advanced side trail that dips off the plateau and into the hillside.

OAK TRAILS (4.1K)
INTERMEDIATE / DIAGONAL AND SKATING
Access this loop from the Willard Munger Trail or from the local roads. For such hilly terrain this trail is remarkably level as it curves around the rim of a plateau. As the name implies, there are lots of oak here. The far section of the loop, where it joins with the Grand Portage of the St. Louis, is a little more challenging.

FOR MORE INFORMATION
Jay Cooke State Park
500 E. Highway 210
Carlton MN 55718
(218) 384-4610

Pattison State Park

TRAILHEAD ACCESS
Drive twelve miles south of Superior on Highway 35 (not Interstate 35). Take park road toward campground and continue to ski trailhead.

TOTAL TRAIL: 7K
Groomed Diagonal: 7K   Skating: none   Lit: none

PASS REQUIREMENTS
• Wisconsin state park vehicle permit. One hour permits ($3), day permits ($5 Wisconsin residents, $7 non-Wisconsin residents) and season permits ($18 Wisconsin residents, $25 non-Wisconsin residents) all available at park office.

TRAILHEAD FACILITIES
Bathroom one-half mile from trailhead.

WHAT MAKES IT UNIQUE
For an extra adventure, ski in to the campsites on the Orange Loop for a night of winter camping. Check at the park office for details.

INTERPRETIVE FEATURE
This trail system gives you a flavor of a different sort of forest than the North Shore. Large basswoods and oaks mix in with the stands of maple. In the winter it's hard to tell these trees apart, especially since their bark is all similar, but with some practice you can do it on the fly.

RED LOOP (2.4K)

EASIER

This mostly level loop starts off in the campground, passes some maintenance buildings, then enters a nice maple and oak forest. At the halfway point there is an overlook of the Black River valley.

BLUE LOOP (3.5K)

INTERMEDIATE

This winding, relatively easy loop takes you clockwise through a quiet and remote corner of the park. The last half of the loop runs along the Black River, with nice views into the valley. Watch for extra large basswood trees and white pine along the trail.

ORANGE LOOP (1K)

INTERMEDIATE

This short loop has plenty of turns and short hills through pockets of birch and fir. A shelter at the far end of the loop marks the entrance to three backpack campsites on the Black River just above Little Manitou Falls (there are outhouses available by the campsites). These are used only infrequently in winter.

FOR MORE INFORMATION
Park Superintendent
6294 S. State Road 35, Superior WI 54880
(715) 399-3111

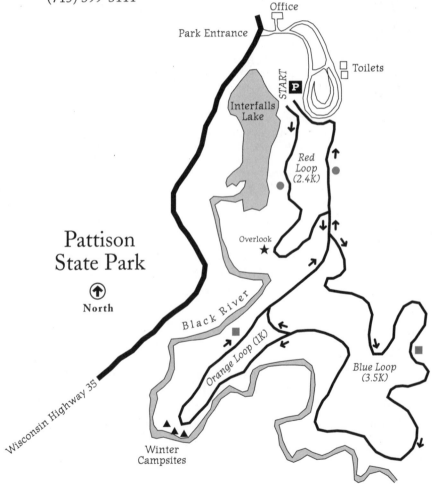

Superior Municipal Forest

TRAILHEAD ACCESS
There are two trailheads: (1) Take 28th Street one mile west
from Tower Avenue. Parking lot is on south side of road, marked
with a sign; (2) Continue on 28th Street until it turns into Billings
Drive. Follow Billings Drive for about two miles to the parking
lot on the left with the ski trail signage.

TOTAL TRAIL: 28K
Groomed Diagonal: 28K   Skating: 28K   Lit: none

PASS REQUIREMENTS
• Day passes ($4) and season passes ($20) available at trailheads.
  Passes required for ages 16 and older; senior discount
  available.

TRAILHEAD FACILITIES
Bathrooms and warming hut at 28th Street trailhead.

SNOW CONDITIONS (715) 394-0299

WHAT MAKES IT UNIQUE
Wide variety of terrain within the country's second largest
municipal forest. The system is ranked as one of Wisconsin's best
cross-country ski trails. The trails are groomed quite wide, so
both skate skiers and classic skiers have plenty of room.

INTERPRETIVE FEATURE
The hills you ski on here are the sides of river valleys carved
when the St. Louis River was a raging stream pouring into a Lake
Superior that was lower than it is today. When the eastern end
of Lake Superior rebounded after the glaciers melted, the lake
flooded the western end, creating the fingers of water that make
up St. Louis Bay, including Kimball's Bay.

RED TRAILS—INNER AND OUTER (3K)
EASY

This is a wide, level warm-up trail, great for families and first-
time skiers. Towering pines give this loop a cozy feel. Both the
inner and outer trail lead from one "island" of white pines to another; these "islands" are on ground that is just a few feet higher
than the "sea" of alder, which are on lower, wetter ground.

Superior Municipal Forest

BLUE TRAIL (2K)
ADVANCED
There are so many fun ups and downs on this trail it feels much longer than 2K. Nice boreal forest and wild hills distinguish this short section from the rest of the trails in the Superior Municipal Forest.

GREEN TRAILS (INNER AND OUTER) (5K)
INTERMEDIATE
This network of trails runs through fields and open woods, zooming down to cross the occasional stream and then up the other side. Although all trails are two-way, most people take these trails counterclockwise (as indicated by the arrows posted on the trails).

The trails on the north and west sides take you into more ambitious terrain, with hills and turns, but for the most part this is family-friendly and fun.

YELLOW LOOP (10K)
ADVANCED

This is rated as advanced primarily because of the distance involved rather than the difficulty of the terrain. There are some serious downhills followed by grunting uphills on the eastern side of the loop, as the trail descends into valleys of the streams that empty into the St. Louis River estuary. Almost all of these downward swoops can be bypassed with side loops. Take the Cedar Point spur trail and you can get out onto Kimball's Bay for some skate skiing if the conditions are right. Settle into a zen-like groove on the return side of the loop, as the terrain and forest hardly changes for over 2K.

PURPLE TRAIL (6K)
ADVANCED

Two-thirds of the Purple Trail is along the snowmobile trail which cuts through the Forest, so be prepared to share this loop with snowmobiles. In the shared section the diagonal trail is either not set or gets quickly erased by the snowmobiles. You'll get right to the edge of Kimball's and Pokegama Bay on this trail… it's hard to imagine these shallow, quiet bays are actually considered to be part of Lake Superior. As the eastern third is the only part not shared with snowmobiles, this trail is best suited just for skate skiing.

FOR MORE INFORMATION
Superior Parks and Recreation Department
1407 Hammond Avenue
Superior WI 54880
(715) 394-0270

Duluth City Parks

Total Trail: 47K

Great Minnesota Ski Pass required.

Scattered across the rugged hills of Duluth is some of the finest urban skiing anywhere, period. In addition to the other options in this chapter, five different city parks await your sampling, ranging from the short but sweet racer's loop at Chester Bowl to the diverse network of trails at Lester Park, from the backcountry of Magney-Snively to the your-own-backyard feel of Piedmont.

Grooming is regular and professional, by a Pisten-Bully groomer. The trailheads have few facilities, but are all within a mile of whatever you might need. The Lester Park trails have five kilometers of trail lit until 11pm each night.

Snow conditions hotline
(218) 624-3062

For more information
Parks and Recreation
12 East Fourth Street
Duluth, MN 55805
(218) 723-3337

Magney-Snively

TRAILHEAD ACCESS
Take Interstate 35 to Boundary Avenue exit. Drive 2.5 miles on Skyline Parkway (past Spirit Mountain recreation area), following the road signs for "Magney ski area." Parking lot is on left side at end of plowed road; trailhead is on right side of road.

TOTAL TRAIL: 14K
Groomed Diagonal: 14K
Skating: 14K   Lit: none

PASS REQUIREMENTS
• Great Minnesota Ski Pass

TRAILHEAD FACILITIES
None

WHAT MAKES IT UNIQUE
Urban old-growth forest. The extensive maple forest and remote-feeling terrain give this in-town ski area a terrific wilderness feel.

INTERPRETIVE FEATURE
If you like the wild places of the region, here is a place to give thanks. This park is named after two of the critical early advocates for both city and state parks along the North Shore. Judge Clarence R. Magney was a mayor of Duluth and a Minnesota supreme court justice who devoted much personal energy to the protection of local lands and landmarks. Samuel F. Snively was also a mayor of Duluth but is known today as the father of Skyline Drive; he started the east end at Seven Bridges Road in 1899, donated his own land and money, and was even known to work alongside the crews.

FULL LOOP (7.5K)
INTERMEDIATE
After a 0.5 K uphill ski on the access trail you enter the most wild, natural and remote of Duluth's ski trails. The trail is marked by long, sometimes steep climbs and smooth, glorious downhills. There is a cutoff that allows you to shorten the loop to 5.5K, but ski the full loop's 1.5K section to Ely Peak and you will gain a beautiful view of the valley below (total of 8.4K).

The ski trail crosses a snowmobile trail (actually Skyline Drive, unplowed in winter) and jogs to the right. You'll ski a very short ways alongside the snowmobile trail, then resume the ski trail in the woods.

BARDONS PEAK LOOP (3.1K)

INTERMEDIATE

Soon after joining the main loop from the 0.5K access trail, you will reach the Bardons Peak Loop juncture. You can extend your outing with this loop and its tremendous overlook view of Duluth, Superior and the St. Louis River valley below. Climb up into maple woods and descend into ash swamps before rejoining the main trail.

Piedmont

TRAILHEAD ACCESS
From the "Seven Corners" intersection (U.S. 53), take Piedmont Avenue two blocks and turn left on Hutchinson Road. Take Hutchinson Road 0.7 miles to small parking lot on the left side of road, near the corner of Adirondack Street.

TOTAL TRAIL: 6K
Groomed Diagonal: 6K   Skating: 6K   Lit: none

PASS REQUIREMENTS
• Great Minnesota Ski Pass

TRAILHEAD FACILITIES
None

WHAT MAKES IT UNIQUE
Homespun flavor. This is a trail with character, built by Piedmont resident Jerry Nowak, and then turned over to the city for management. The clever signs along the trail keep you laughing.

INTERPRETIVE FEATURE
This is almost all second-growth forest, but with a lot more willow than you might expect. Dropping over the edge of Duluth gabbro onto the expert trails brings you into older trees.

MAIN LOOP (4K)
EASY AND INTERMEDIATE
Clever signs urge you on past small dips through a nicely mixed deciduous forest as you climb very gradually to a dramatic over-look, one of the best on Duluth trails. The trail is generally well-suited for beginners, but watch out for the two exceptions. A short, fun intermediate loop at the end can be bypassed by a 50-foot cutoff ("Chicken Loop"), and a swooping hill at the end can be bypassed by turning right at the "Piker's Peak" sign. Although skate skiing is allowed here, the lane is pretty narrow.

EXPERT LOOP (2K)
ADVANCED
This is a new addition to the Piedmont trails and provides about 2K of steep hills and sharp turns on the edge of the bluff. Some nice pine trees add to the exciting atmosphere.

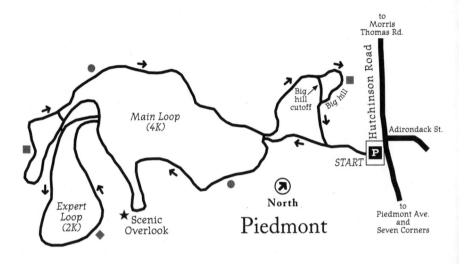

to
Morris
Thomas Rd.

Hutchinson Road

Main Loop
(4K)

Big
hill
cutoff

Big hill

Adirondack St.

START

P

North

Piedmont

Expert
Loop
(2K)

★ Scenic
Overlook

to
Piedmont Ave.
and
Seven Corners

Inuit snow names

All snow is not the same. When the snow reaches the ground, it changes
as the wind and weather shape it. The Inuit people of the Kobuk Valley in
Alaska have named and described the following types of snow:

Falling snow .... *Annui*

Snow that collects on trees .... *Qali*

Snow on the ground .... *Api*

Depth hoar .... *Pukak*

Wind-beaten snow .... *Upsik*

Sun crust .... *Siqoqtaoq*

❄

Chester Bowl

TRAILHEAD ACCESS
Take Skyline Parkway to the Chester Bowl Ski Area, either east from Kenwood Avenue or west from College Street and 19th Avenue East.

TOTAL TRAIL: 3K
Groomed Diagonal: 3K   Skating: 3K   Lit: 0.75K

PASS REQUIREMENTS
• Great Minnesota Ski Pass

TRAILHEAD FACILITIES
Chalet, bathrooms.

WHAT MAKES IT UNIQUE
Wild and wooly in-town ski area specifically for advanced skiers and racers. With downhill skiing and ski jumping available, Chester Bowl can be a complete ski outing.

INTERPRETIVE FEATURE
Underneath the ridgetop, from which this trail overlooks Lake Superior, is one of the oldest of the lava flows that make up the North Shore today and the westernmost exposure of the North Shore Volcanics group. The bedrock gets younger and younger as you go up the shore. The youngest flows (20 million years younger!) are found in the vicinity of Tofte. Beyond Tofte, the flows start getting older again, with the oldest flows in the area of Grand Portage.

MAIN LOOP (3K)

ADVANCED / LIT ON REQUEST

This is a course designed for racers and advanced skiers. There are serious downhills and difficult turns. After a level start across a soccer field and into the woods, you will cross a bridge over Chester Creek and start climbing. As if you're on a roller coaster, you will ski up and down and around tight corners. About halfway is an open field with a 120° view of Lake Superior and Park Point. After the field you descend into a mixed maple forest before one last climb up above the Chester Bowl chairlift for a final run back to where you began three hairy kilometers before. The first 0.75K can be lit on request at the chalet.

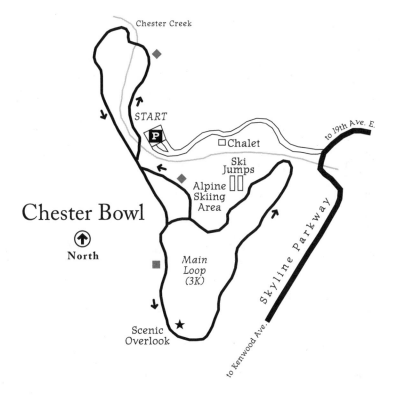

Snow crystals

Snow crystals seem to all look different, but they do come in distinct forms. All flakes are made up of one or more of the following elements: hexagonal plate, stellar or dendrite (both like the child's paper snowflake), column, needle, and asymmetrical. Each crystal form represents a different set of climatic conditions. When the weather is unsettled, individual crystal types can join to form unique combination crystals. Sometimes the crystal form disappears entirely, beaten up from frost and rime; this is known as graupel. ✳

Hartley Field

TRAILHEAD ACCESS
There are two trailheads: (1) Take Fairmont Road two blocks from Woodland Avenue, or (2) Take Hartley Road 0.3 miles from four-way stop at Arrowhead Road.

TOTAL TRAIL: 5K
Groomed Diagonal: 5K   Skating: none   Lit: none

PASS REQUIREMENTS
• Great Minnesota Ski Pass

TRAILHEAD FACILITIES
None

WHAT MAKES IT UNIQUE
This is a "multiple use" city park; expect to see signs of the playful fifth grader or the snowshoeing UMD student. Hartley Nature Center is continually expanding its educational offerings as Duluth's only nature center.

INTERPRETIVE FEATURE
In a tight space there is real diversity of habitat types, from upland maple to lowland ash, plus pine plantations and more. Can you pick out the plantations from the natural growth? Watch for trees all of one type (like white spruce) in relatively neat rows; those are the plantations. The mixed forests of aspen and birch with scattered white pine are natural growth.

INNER LOOP (2K)
EASY
This loop is largely easy going for the beginner, with just enough hills to provide for the beginner's "learning experiences" (also known as falls). The true beginning skier should start at the Hartley Road trailhead to avoid a big uphill on the access trail from the Fairmont trailhead.

OUTER LOOP (3K)
INTERMEDIATE
This is a wilder ride, especially on the south side, with hills both to climb and glide down. There are nice views of Hartley Hill along the north side of the loop. A connector trail to the inner loop adds in some extra, optional thrills, but watch out as the junction to this connector trail is in a turn on a downhill run. The

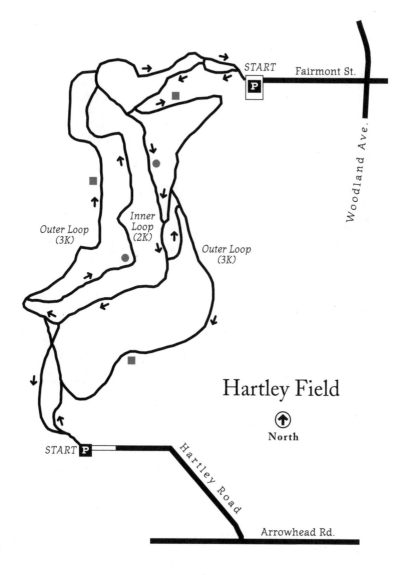

Fairmont St.

START

Woodland Ave.

Outer Loop
(3K)

Inner
Loop
(2K)

Outer Loop
(3K)

Hartley Field

⊕
North

START

Hartley Road

Arrowhead Rd.

downhill at the southern end of the loop is particularly challenging, with a big right turn halfway down. You can skip this downhill by taking a skier-packed cutoff on the right.

Lester Park

TRAILHEAD ACCESS
There are three trailheads: (1) Take Lester River Road 100 yards up from Superior Street to large parking lot on left; (2) Take Seven Bridges Road (Occidental Boulevard) to roadside parking about one mile from Superior Street; (3) Take Seven Bridges Road to the Lakeside Chalet, about two miles from Superior Street.

TOTAL TRAIL: 18K
Groomed Diagonal: 18K   Skating: 18K   Lit: 3.4K

PASS REQUIREMENTS
• Great Minnesota Ski Pass

TRAILHEAD FACILITIES
None at Superior Street. Bathrooms, warming room at Lakeside Chalet.

WHAT MAKES IT UNIQUE
Lots of skiing on the edge of the city makes for a popular trail, especially at night.

INTERPRETIVE FEATURE
The dramatic white pines along the lower loop by Amity Creek are a remnant of a forest that covered much of this area. In contrast, the upper trails are in a relatively young second-growth forest of aspen and birch. These trails give you both extremes of forest management, from the untouched to the recently reforested.

ACCESS TRAIL (1.4K)

INTERMEDIATE

From the Lester River Road trailhead, cross the bridge, then climb through majestic white pine after crossing the open field. The first climb is pretty steep. Lighting may be added to this trail. On the downhill run back into the open park field you will glide by huge pines and the scenic river—a real North Woods treat!

INNER/BEGINNER LOOP (3.4K)

EASY

This is a very popular 3.4K loop, which divides into a 1.7K southern loop that is a little hillier (one long, gradual climb and one long, gradual downhill) and a 1.7K northern loop that is a little flatter. The wide trail leads through an open forest of birch and aspen. A few short dips keep you on your toes. The northern loop

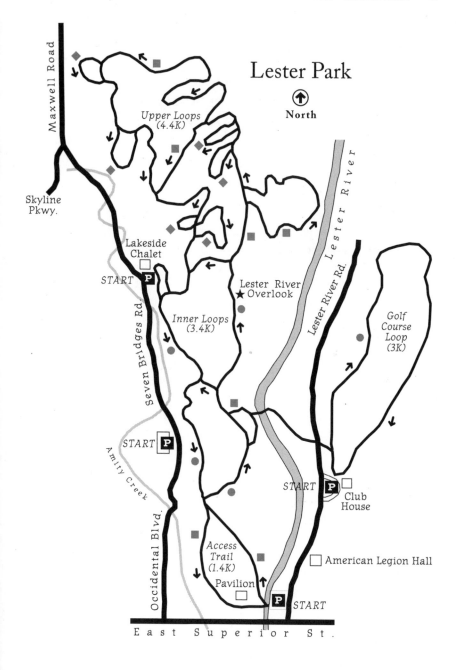

Maxwell Road

Lester Park

⊕
North

Upper Loops
(4.4K)

Skyline
Pkwy.

Lester River

Lester River Rd.

Lakeside
Chalet

START **P**

Lester River
★ Overlook

Golf
Course
Loop
(3K)

Inner Loops
(3.4K)

Seven Bridges Rd

START **P**

START **P** ☐
Club
House

Amity Creek

☐ American Legion Hall

Access
Trail
(1.4K)

Pavilion

Occidental Blvd.

☐ **P** *START*

E a s t   S u p e r i o r   S t .

has a nice overlook of the Lester River. The loop is lit every night until 11pm and mornings from 5am to daylight. Expect to share the trail with speedy skate skiers and leisurely families. Most people start this loop from the Seven Bridges Road parking lot.

UPPER LOOPS (4.4K PLUS SIDE LOOPS)
INTERMEDIATE AND ADVANCED / TO BE PARTLY LIT

This is really two trails. The main trail is 4.4K of intermediate skiing through mixed forest. It's a gradual climb into level terrain, followed by a bit of a roller coaster ride down. You'll get away from the crowds on this loop. You can add a nice, relatively level 1.2K intermediate side loop on the way up.

The Upper Loops can also be an expert trail by adding the six advanced side loops, each about 0.5K. Each advanced side loop has both a steep climb and descent, not necessarily in that order. If you do all the side loops, this section ends up being around 9K. Caution: If you're not up for the hills and turns, watch out at intersections "I" and "J"; the intermediate trail goes left while the advanced trail goes straight ahead.

GOLF COURSE (3K, PLUS 0.7K ACCESS FROM INNER LOOP)
EASY

The open, rolling terrain of the Lester Park Golf Course makes for a radically different skiing experience than the rest of Lester Park. This is not lit, but is skiable at night by full moon (at your own risk). Nice views of Lake Superior from the upper parts. You can park at the golf course clubhouse, 0.4 miles up Lester River Road from Superior Street, or ski to the golf course along the connector trail which crosses the river on a bridge, then crosses Lester River Road.

Spirit Mountain

TRAILHEAD ACCESS
Take Skyline Drive from Interstate 35 (Exit #249) and follow signs to Spirit Mountain Recreation Area. Stay on Skyline Drive past entrance to downhill area on left. Watch for turn on right side marked "Cross Country."

TOTAL TRAIL: 22K
Groomed Diagonal: 22K   Skating: 22K   Lit: 2K

PASS REQUIREMENTS
• Day passes ($7, or $4 after 2pm) and season passes ($50/adult, $30/child, $145/family) for sale at trailhead chalet.

TRAILHEAD FACILITIES
Chalet, bathrooms, snacks, equipment rentals.

SNOW CONDITIONS HOTLINE (800) 642-6377

WHAT MAKES IT UNIQUE
This trail system is professionally groomed daily and is far from the moderating impact of Lake Superior weather, so it often provides the best and most consistent skiing conditions in Duluth.

INTERPRETIVE FEATURE
There is a wonderful variety of deciduous trees here. Although there are many sugar maple, there are also more unusual trees like basswood, large yellow birch and ironwood. You may see the distinctive seeds of the ironwood in their tan envelopes scattering across the top of the snow.

All loops start and end at the log warming hut, a 0.5K ski in from the chalet, where tickets and refreshments are for sale and ski rental is available. All trails are groomed wide for skate skiing with diagonal tracks on both sides, which is nice for skiing with a friend.

ERIK JUDEEN TRAIL (1K)
BEGINNER
Easy loop popular with families and for instruction. Follow the green dots on a gradual climb to a sharp turn, then wind easily back to the warming hut.

CHARLIE BANKS TRAIL (3K)
INTERMEDIATE
This loop starts off tricky and then eases off. "Dennis' Demise" is the biggest hill on the intermediate trails and may give the begin-

George Hovland Trail (11K)

Pete Fosseide Trail
(5K)

*Charlie
Banks Trail
(3K)*

Erik
Judeen
Trail
(1K)

Hut

P

↑START

Nordic Center

*Larry
Sorenson
Trail
(2K)*
(Campground Loop)

Skyline Drive

North

to Magney-Snively
Ski Area

to I-35

Spirit Mountain

ning skier a safe scare. Otherwise, this is a gently rolling trail, marked by yellow dots, that stays on top of the plateau.

PETE FOSSEIDE TRAIL (5K)

INTERMEDIATE

A little more challenging overall than the Charlie Banks Trail, this loop also brings you into a more diverse forest. Following the blue dots, this trail takes you off of a plateau, with a series of downhills right at the start. The terrain then levels out as you circle around the backside of the plateau and return to the warming hut.

GEORGE HOVLAND TRAIL (11K)
INTERMEDIATE TO EXPERT

This loop is for the ambitious, experienced skier. Whoever laid it out managed to find every hill and turn available. You will double back on your tracks numerous times, having skied 2K but only having gone a few meters forward. If you get tired from the length or the hills, watch for near intersections with the 5K loop where you can bail out. You can also cut off two loops with about 2K of trail when you're two-thirds through.

LARRY SORENSON TRAIL (CAMPGROUND LOOP) (2K)
BEGINNER / LIT

This easy loop through the summer campground is lit for night skiing. The loop starts and ends with gradual downhills. The gentle climb in between has nice views through the trees of the St. Louis River valley. Beginners should start here before heading up to the warming hut and the other loops.

ASSOCIATED LODGING

The Spirit Mountain Villas are within a snowball's throw both of these trails and the downhill runs. Contact the number below for information.

FOR MORE INFORMATION

Spirit Mountain
9500 Spirit Mountain Place
Duluth MN 55810
(218) 628-2891
spiritmt@cp.duluth.mn.us
www.aminews.com/SpiritMt

Legends of Skiing

The trails at Spirit Mountain pay tribute to the legends of Northeastern Minnesota skiing. For example, Erik Judeen and Pete Fosseide were buddies who established Duluth's first ski trails, in Chester Bowl. Pete won the 1938 three-day, 153-mile ski race from Duluth to St. Paul.

Charlie Banks developed the trails now known as Korkki Nordic Ski Center in the 1950s. George Hovland, who developed both these trails and those at Snowflake Nordic Center, was on the 1952 Olympic ski team in Oslo. ❄

Rock Hill/Bagley Nature Area

TRAILHEAD ACCESS
Take St. Marie Street from Woodland Avenue to the Rock Hill/ Bagley Nature Area parking lot near Oakland Apartments.

TOTAL TRAIL: 2.7K
Groomed Diagonal: 2.7K   Skating: none   Lit: none

PASS REQUIREMENTS
None. Parking meters at trailhead enforced 8am to 8pm, Monday through Friday; 25¢ for each 30 minutes.

TRAILHEAD FACILITIES
None

WHAT MAKES IT UNIQUE
A great asset for students is also available for community use.

INTERPRETIVE FEATURE
This area is also known as the "Sugarbush" because of the active demonstration of traditional syruping run in the spring for educational purposes. Sugar maples dominate these trails, especially the eastern loop.

WEST LOOP (1.2K)

INTERMEDIATE

This is the more challenging of the two loops as you ski around Rock Hill, a former downhill ski area. The trail climbs for a long time through maple forest with some nice paper birch mixed in. Where the trail crosses a closed road to the top of Rock Hill, stop for some winter tree identification: there is maple, oak and basswood here—can you pick them out? A downhill run takes you back to Rock Pond.

EAST LOOP (1.5K)

EASIER

Take a quick loop through UMD's maple sugarbush. In March and April, if the skiing is still good, you might find sap bags on the trees and school groups learning about maple sugaring. This is mostly level terrain except for the section along Tischer Creek, where you will have to be able to herringbone or sidestep. If you feel like you're skiing through someone's backyard here, it's because you almost are; please stay on the trail. One-way signs direct you through some potentially confusing intersections.

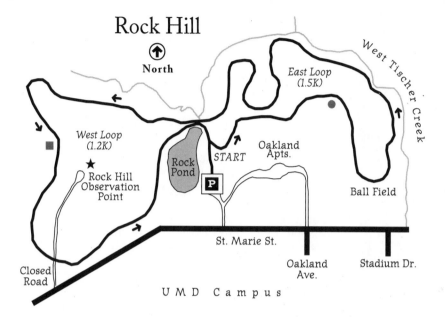

FOR MORE INFORMATION
UMD Outdoor Program
121 SpHC, 10 University Drive
Duluth MN 55812
(218) 726-6533

Snowflake Nordic Center

TRAILHEAD ACCESS
Take Rice Lake Road 0.5 mile north of Arrowhead Road.
Entrance road is shared with tennis club.

TOTAL TRAIL: 13.5K
Groomed Diagonal: 13.5K   Skating: 13.5K   Lit: 6K

PASS REQUIREMENTS
• Day passes ($7.50 or $3 after 6pm) and season passes
($100/person, $150/family before November 4; or
$125/person, $200/family after November 4) for sale at
trailhead.

TRAILHEAD FACILITIES
Chalet with bathrooms, changing rooms, sauna, wax room and
fireplace. Rentals, beverages and snacks available.

WHAT MAKES IT UNIQUE
Professional grooming and facilities available right in town.
Snowflake is frequented by ski racers and hosts the local high-
school ski teams for practices as well as races.

INTERPRETIVE FEATURE
Note the scattered aspen, birch and pine with wide spreading
limbs. These first grew in an open field, where their limbs could
reach *out* for sunlight. The younger trees have grown all together
and are reaching *up* for their light.

EASIEST LOOP (1K)

LIT

This easy loop rolls through the flats right near the chalet. Start
the kids off here and someday they'll want to do the big loops too.

INTERMEDIATE LOOP (5K)

LIT

This loop is trickiest at the start and finish, with some short, steep
climbs to challenge any skier. However, the middle "half" is relatively flat, with the main challenge coming from tight curves—
this is a nice stretch to focus on technique. The lighting is effective
if a little unromantic, with power lines strung from tree to tree. A
cutoff after the 3K mark lets you skip a 0.5K level loop. Ignore the
other lights and trails and settle in for the curvy "here and now."

MOST DIFFICULT LOOP (7.5K)

If you're into getting from Point A to Point B, this trail is not for you and might in fact drive you crazy. But if you're into the aesthetics of a well-groomed trail and a well-designed curve, check this out. Don't even try to keep your bearings. This loop squeezes a great variety of terrain out of a tight area, beginning with some steep ups and downs curving around a log hut, where a marked cutoff brings you right back to the chalet. If the first hills intimidated you, hold on; you've made it through the only truly advanced stretch of the loop. The rest is classic intermediate terrain and leads eventually into some nice woods, both birch and evergreen. An unmarked cutoff about two-thirds of the way through allows you to cut off about 1.5K of the trail.

FOR MORE INFORMATION
Snowflake Nordic Center
4348 Rice Lake Road, Duluth MN 55811
(218) 726-1550

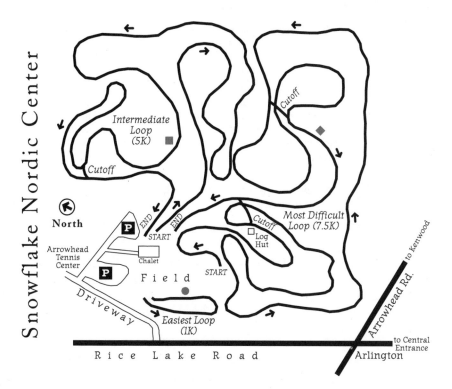

Boulder Lake

TRAILHEAD ACCESS
Boulder Lake is 18 miles north of Duluth. Take Highway 4 north to the Island Lake Inn, then turn north on the Boulder Dam Road. There are three trailheads along Boulder Dam Road:
(1) Bear Paw/Blue Ox trailhead, with its intermediate trails;
(2) Rolling Pin trailhead by Nordberg Road, with advanced trails;
(3) Otter Run trailhead at Boulder Dam, at the end of the road, with the easy Otter Run trail. All trails are connected.

TOTAL TRAIL: 13K
Groomed diagonal: 13K   Skating: none   Lit: none
Watch for 5K to 10K of additional trail opening soon!

PASS REQUIREMENTS
None

TRAILHEAD FACILITIES
Outhouse at Rolling Pin and Otter Run trailheads. Warming shack at Rolling Pin occasionally open.

SNOW CONDITIONS HOTLINE (218) 722-5642, EXT. 2852

WHAT MAKES IT UNIQUE
These trails are the result of a partnership between Minnesota Power, the State of Minnesota and St. Louis County. They are built on Minnesota Power, state and county land near the shores of Boulder Lake, a reservoir for Minnesota Power's hydroelectric power generation system.

INTERPRETIVE FEATURE
The trails from the Rolling Pin trailhead crisscross a well-formed esker. Eskers are a landform made of gravel deposited in a river underneath a melting glacier. They are a common source of well-sorted gravel, as demonstrated by the gravel pit at the western end of Ridge Runner.

ROLLING PIN / RIDGE RUNNER / TIMBER CRUISER (2.2K)
INTERMEDIATE TO EXPERT

These three trails form a figure eight using a glacial esker for the "cross." Because of the one-way markings, most skiers will ski all three. Rolling Pin winds you around to the start of Ridge Runner, which traces the top of an esker. Timber Cruiser starts with a big downhill coming off of the esker.

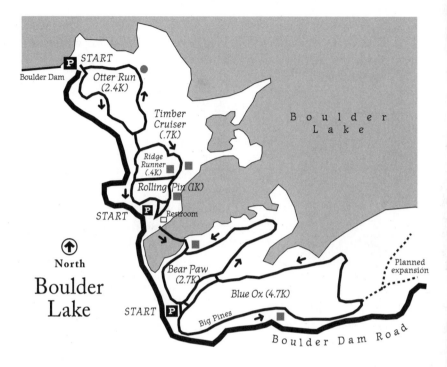

START

Boulder Dam

Otter Run (2.4K)

Timber Cruiser (.7K)

B o u l d e r
L a k e

Ridge Runner (.4K)

Rolling Pin (1K)

START

Restroom

North

Boulder Lake

Planned expansion

Bear Paw (2.7K)

Blue Ox (4.7K)

START

Big Pines

B o u l d e r   D a m   R o a d

OTTER RUN (2.4K)

BEGINNER TO INTERMEDIATE

This loop trail leads to Boulder Dam itself and the piney shores of Boulder Lake Reservoir. The forest is incredibly diverse here, with thick, old white pine at the western end, plus maple, large-toothed aspen and ash. The entire trail is level and easy going. Boulder Lake Reservoir drains into Island Lake through Otter Creek, thus the name of this trail. Beginners will want to access this loop from the parking lot at Boulder Dam, to avoid the hills at the Rolling Pin trailhead.

BEAR PAW (2.7K)

INTERMEDIATE

Access this double tracked trail either from the Bear Paw/Blue Ox trailhead or by heading across Boulder Lake from the warming hut, the trail across the frozen expanse marked by trees stuck in the snow. This mostly level loop takes you through a young aspen forest with occasional patches of old white pine. Occasional views of the open stretches of Boulder Lake keep the skiing interesting. With the side-by-side tracks, this is a nice place to ski and talk with a friend.

"Popping" Birches

It's a cold you can feel deep inside, your breath bearing icy knives into the recesses of your lungs. Luckily, it's just a walk up the driveway before turning in. A dangerous cold—with the night sky so clear it will get even colder. Tonight will be a far cry from the relative warmth of the afternoon, when winter sun warmed the hillsides and the birch trees, melting the sap within. Now, with the return of the real cold, the sap freezes again—and freezes fast. The freeze cracks open the side of the birch with a muffled gunshot. A muffled "what's that?" and then you remember: it is February, the moon of the popping trees. ❄

BLUE OX (4.7K)
INTERMEDIATE

Babe the Blue Ox was Paul Bunyan's helper in logging the mighty pines. This trail shows the "before" and "after" of Babe's work. The first half of this loop rolls gently through a wonderful white pine forest. The second half is all vigorous regrowth of aspen and birch. The trail is double-tracked and not as difficult as the rating implies, so it's a good place to take an advanced beginner for his or her first big loop.

FOR MORE INFORMATION
Minnesota Power
Environmental Division
30 West Superior Street
Duluth MN 55802
(218) 723-3977

Boulder Lake Environmental
Center (218) 721-3372

Korkki Nordic Ski Center

TRAILHEAD ACCESS
Take Homestead Road (County Road 42) 2.5 miles north from milepost 14.9 on Highway 61 Expressway, to left turn at Korkki Road. Go west on Korkki Road (County Road 43) for 0.5 miles to Nordic Center entrance on right.

TOTAL TRAIL: 11K
Groomed Diagonal: 11K   Skating: none   Lit: none

PASS REQUIREMENTS
None. Donation box at trailhead. Suggested donation of $3–$5. Annual membership available ($15/family, $10 individual).

TRAILHEAD FACILITIES
Chalet with wood stove and changing room. Outhouse.

WHAT MAKES IT UNIQUE
Privately maintained trail with lots of history and character, preserving traditional single-track, classical skiing and a sense of skiing community. Has been called "possibly the prettiest trail on the North Shore."

INTERPRETIVE FEATURE
These are truly "Charlie's Trails," as they are affectionately called by those in the know. Charlie Banks is one of the legendary figures of Duluth skiing, and built these trails himself in 1955 on public land in his "backyard." The Korkki of Korkki Road and Korkki Nordic Ski Center was Charlie's father-in-law, who homesteaded here. Korkki Nordic Ski Center was formed in 1993 as a nonprofit organization dedicated to maintaining this premiere example of traditional nordic skiing.

MAIN LOOP (10K)
INTERMEDIATE TO ADVANCED
This is one long loop with cutoff options along the way to make smaller loops of 6K and 7.5K. Single-tracked and narrow, with exciting hills where you can't see the bottom and throw caution to the wind…but it all works out fine.

FIRST 6K
INTERMEDIATE
The 6K cutoff keeps you on intermediate terrain, gradually climbing through mixed forest and ash swamps, then returning on a wonderful gradual downhill run that makes you feel like a champion skier. There are two especially challenging parts of the downhill run, fun rides up and down along a river bank. Most skiers

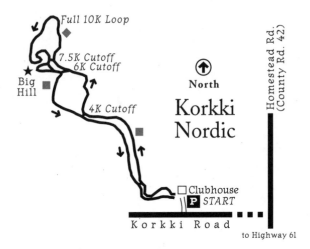

stay on the main trail over these features, but beginning skiers can avoid these on side trails. Cutoffs at 1K and 4K allow for a shorter run.

BRYAN'S LOOP
ADVANCED

Skiers choosing the "whole enchilada" will experience more challenging terrain, with some sharp turns on steep hills. There are some nice beaver ponds and piney ridges (known as "Wolf Kill Ridge") back here too. The middle third of the loop is relatively level and in open woods, but the last third has a hairpin turn and other thrills. The "Iso Maki Big Hill," also available to those who take the 7.5K cutoff, is a steep climb to a great view from the top of inland ridges, and a speedy run down a hill that seems to go on forever. A cutoff is available to those who, for some reason, want to skip the hill.

CAMP LOOP (1K)
EASIER

A new loop, double-tracked and wider than the main loop, is perfect for kids and instructional outings. On some special occasions this loop may be lantern-lit.

FOR MORE INFORMATION
Charlie Banks or Mark Helmer
1711 Korkki Road, Duluth MN 55804 (218) 525-7326

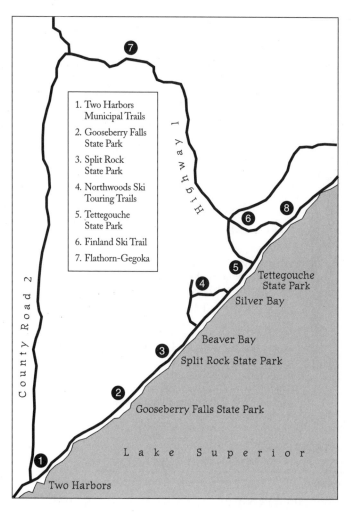

1. Two Harbors
   Municipal Trails
2. Gooseberry Falls
   State Park
3. Split Rock
   State Park
4. Northwoods Ski
   Touring Trails
5. Tettegouche
   State Park
6. Finland Ski Trail
7. Flathorn-Gegoka

Tettegouche
State Park

Silver Bay

Beaver Bay

Split Rock State Park

Gooseberry Falls State Park

Lake   Superior

Two Harbors

Highway 1

County Road 2

Lake County Cross-Country Ski Trails

State parks and volunteers. Skiing Lake County gives you new apprecia-
tion of both. The North Shore state parks stick out on the maps, from
the diverse network at Gooseberry to the deep woods and dramatic
terrain of Tettegouche, with nice facilities to match. But you will find
some little gems tucked into the hills, like Silver Bay's Northwoods Ski
Touring Trail and the Two Harbors system, both maintained by local
volunteers. Away from the shore, on the edge of the Boundary Waters,
you will find the towering pines of Flathorn-Gegoka. Maybe they should
change Lake County's name to "Snow County!"

Two Harbors Municipal Trail

TRAILHEAD ACCESS
Take County Road 2 0.7 miles north of Highway 61 until signed entrance to parking lot on the right side of the road.

TOTAL TRAIL: 8K
Groomed Diagonal: 8K   Skating: 8K   Lit: none

PASS REQUIREMENTS
• Great Minnesota Ski Pass
• Membership in Two Harbors Recreational Trail Club
  recommended ($10/individual, $15/family).

TRAILHEAD FACILITIES
None

WHAT MAKES IT UNIQUE
Right on the edge of town is a gentle, quiet set of ski trails well used and loved by local families.

INTERPRETIVE FEATURE
How does wind affect snow? As the new trails wind in and out of the open areas of the golf course fairway, notice the difference in snow cover. As the wind blows snow into unusual streamlined forms, it also packs the snow and causes it to harden. In fact, the Inuit people, who have lots of open areas and lots of snow, had a different name for the snow as it drifts, *siqoq,* and once it is wind-packed, *upsik.* Chances are you will be able to feel and even hear the difference.

OUTSIDE TRAIL
(4.5K, PLUS 1K ADVANCED SIDE LOOPS)
EASIER

The terrain is gently rolling, with few uphills or downhills. When taken counterclockwise, the first quarter of the trail winds through the new fairways, providing open views. Past the junction with inner trails, about 1K in, the trail enters the woods, leaving the fairways behind. Two side loops of about 0.5K each, the Flood Bay Loop and Lauder's Loop, are for advanced skiers, with quick turns and sharp climbs. Between the two side trails is an ungroomed connector trail leading to Superior Shores resort. A straight portion known as "Dump Road Stretch" brings you to a last, winding section through conifers back to the trailhead. The first 1K will be lit for night skiing if organizers raise the funds.

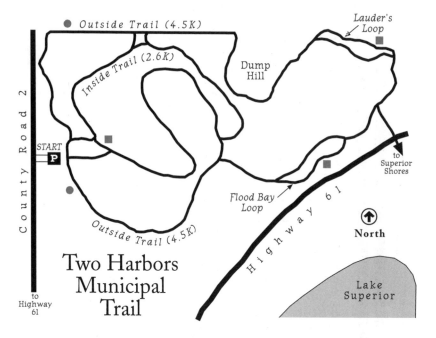

INSIDE TRAIL (2.6K)

INTERMEDIATE

Construction in 1996 of nine more holes on the Two Harbors golf course caused a lot of changes to the layout of the ski trail. This inside loop forms the outline of a "C" as it runs through the strips of woods between the fairways. The open fairways provide an airy feel to your ski. Organizers hope to provide lighting for the south side of the loop, connecting with the first part of the Outside Trail for about 2.6K of lit trail.

FOR MORE INFORMATION
Two Harbors Ski Club
514 15th Avenue
Two Harbors MN 55616
(218) 834-4024

Gooseberry Falls State Park

TRAILHEAD ACCESS
Take Visitor Center/Wayside Rest exit off Highway 61, twelve miles northeast of Two Harbors. Go either to Visitor Center or to Lakeview picnic shelter on lakeshore.

TOTAL TRAIL: 20K
Groomed Diagonal: 20K   Skating: none   Lit: none

PASS REQUIREMENTS
• Great Minnesota Ski Pass
• Minnesota State Parks vehicle permit (only when using Lakeview picnic center trailhead)

TRAILHEAD FACILITIES
Bathrooms, snacks, warming room, gift shop and Visitor Center.

WHAT MAKES IT UNIQUE
Gooseberry is the first big North Shore ski area as you head up the shore. Its diverse terrain and remote trails make it a favorite for daytrippers from the Duluth area.

INTERPRETIVE FEATURE
Each of the waterfalls at Gooseberry falls over different lava flows. The falls below the highway bridge drape over three flows altogether. Away from the river, much of the park is open birch forest, managed by park officials for an open feel that makes skiing a particular pleasure on sunny days.

Lakeside trails

CAMPGROUND LOOP (3.3K)

EASY

Take this trail either direction through the open woods of the lakeshore and campground area. You can start from the Visitor Center area, or if you have a vehicle permit you can start on the 0.3K spur from Lakeview picnic shelter by Agate Beach. The views, of the Gooseberry River valley and the icy Lake Superior shore, are among the most dramatic of all North Shore trails. The trail crosses a park road twice, so you may have to take off your skis or step gingerly across the pavement.

Inland trails

Access these trails from the Visitor Center. A main feeder trail will lead under the highway bridge on the west side of river, with a dramatic view of the Upper Falls. This feeder trail is scheduled to open in 1998-99. During construction of the new bridge, inquire at the visitors center for connecting information.

BIRCH HILL LOOP (3.4K)
INTERMEDIATE

If you are coming from the trailhead on the west side of Highway 61, you will take a 0.7K access trail to this remote-feeling loop. Watch for the deer "excloser" just past the junction with the trail down to Fifth Falls. After a steep climb to the open birch woods, get ready for a fun, gradual 1.2K downhill run. When you finally have to kick again, it will be in a nice mixed open forest.

CENTER FIELDS LOOP (5.4K)
INTERMEDIATE

Cross the bridge over the Gooseberry River (shared with snowmobiles) and enter this open country of spruce and birch. The main counterclockwise loop is 4.4K of trail from the bridge. It's great for relaxed cruising, especially on a sunny day when you can stop at the shelter and bask in the rays. The two-way cutoff up the middle of the loop adds variety. Take off from this main loop onto either of the sections below for a full adventure. Enjoy a break at the Fifth Falls bridge, but do take off your skis before heading down.

Photo: RUDI HARGESHEIMER

Warmer by the lake

Is the North Shore the "Arctic Riviera?" Believe it or not, North Shore communities can be the warmest places in Minnesota on some deeply cold mornings. Lake Superior has an average temperature of 39 degrees Fahrenheit. In summer, the lake acts like a big ice cube and keeps us cool; in winter, it acts like a big radiator and keeps us warm. ❄

EASTERN HILLS (5.8K)
INTERMEDIATE TO ADVANCED

Head out into this section, and if you are comfortable with some hills and turns, forget about the maps that show up every few hundred meters and just follow your curiosity up and down and around these hills. You won't get lost, but you will enjoy diverse country of thick and old woods and the occasional view. One 0.8K section is rated advanced for its tight turns and sharp hills; it also connects with a neighboring lodge. If you make it to the overlook, pull out a snack and enjoy!

Photo: RUDI HARGESHEIMER

Lake Superior freezing over

February and March are the months for icewatchers. The water of Lake Superior is at its coldest in the month of March. Almost every year the shallower or more protected bays of the North Shore will freeze over during the late winter, but some years it is frozen as far as the eye can see. And once every twenty years or so, the whole lake freezes over. It takes a combination of a long-term cold winter, a serious cold snap and relatively calm seas. This happened in 1978, 1994 and (some say) again in 1996. Keep an eye out: perhaps the next ice age is here! ❋

VALLEY TRAILS (2.1K)
INTERMEDIATE

If the skiing is fast, this section can be scary. Downhill runs scoot you down to the banks of the Gooseberry, where you will cruise past some huge cedar trees. The climb back up the river bank is fairly long and steep.

FOR MORE INFORMATION
Gooseberry Falls State Park
1300 Highway 61 East
Two Harbors MN 55616
(218) 834-3855

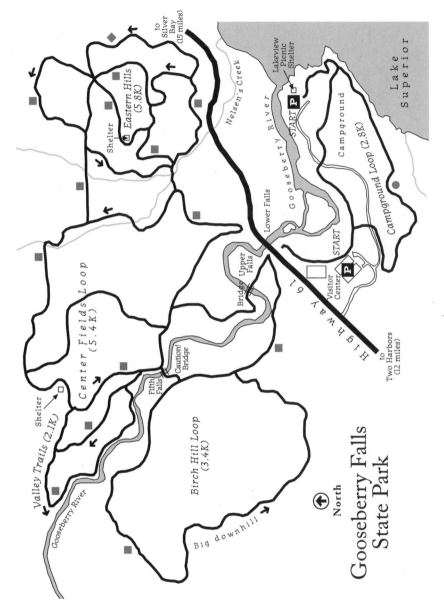

Gooseberry Falls
State Park

North

Lake Superior

to Silver Bay
(15 miles)

Nelsen's Creek

Lakeview Picnic Shelter

START

Gooseberry River

Campground

Campground Loop (2.8K)

Eastern Hills
(5.8K)

Shelter

Lower Falls

Center Fields Loop
(5.4K)

Upper Falls

Bridge

START

Visitor Center

Highway 61

to Two Harbors
(12 miles)

Valley Trails (2.1K)

Shelter

Caution! Bridge

Fifth Falls

Gooseberry River

Birch Hill Loop
(3.4K)

Big downhill

Split Rock Lighthouse State Park

TRAILHEAD ACCESS
Go to Split Rock Lighthouse State Park, 21 miles northeast of Two Harbors on Highway 61. Follow signs to the right past the guard station to parking lot at Trail Center.

TOTAL TRAIL: 12.8K
Groomed Diagonal: 12.8K   Skating: none   Lit: none

PASS REQUIREMENTS
• Great Minnesota Ski Pass
• Minnesota State Parks vehicle permit

TRAILHEAD FACILITIES
Trail Center with bathrooms and indoor picnic facility.

WHAT MAKES IT UNIQUE
Trails right along shore add drama and beauty to your ski.

INTERPRETIVE FEATURE
Split Rock Lighthouse is situated on top of a 124-foot cliff that is composed of diabase. If you are lucky and well dressed, you could experience for yourself one of the main reasons the lighthouse was installed: roaring northeasters of the late shipping season, such as the one in November, 1905, which sank two ships nearby (the *Lafayette* and the *Madeira*). The other main reason for the lighthouse was fog, but ski season and fog season seldom overlap.

LITTLE TWO HARBORS AND DAY HILL TRAILS (4K)
INTERMEDIATE
Your introduction to skiing at Split Rock includes both essential elements of this park's trails: lakeshore skiing and speedy hills. Starting from the Trail Center you can either head up a dead end toward the lighthouse or ski around Day Hill, climbing over 100 feet to get to the rest of the trail system. Don't be tempted into skiing the lakeside portion of the Day Hill trail; steep stairways make it unskiable. The view of the lighthouse from Little Two Harbors, where the ski trail is right on the cobblestone beach, is postcard perfect.

CORUNDUM MINE LOOP (5.1K)
EASY TO INTERMEDIATE
Much of outbound part of this loop follows the old highway, providing smooth skiing at first. Coming back along the lakeshore is a little more exciting. Take at least one of the spur trails towards the lake (but not the Corundum Point Trail) for nice views of the bluffs and lake.

MERRILL LOGGING LOOP (3.4K)
INTERMEDIATE

After carefully crossing Highway 61, you will climb the eastern bank of Split Rock Creek, not to be confused with its bigger sister to the west, the Split Rock River. The second 100-foot-plus climb of the day takes you past a large deer excloser to a junction with the Superior Hiking Trail and then quickly onto the bed of an old logging railroad. This provides a straight shot down for 1K before climbing steeply to a shelter and overlook with a nice view down to the Split Rock River, Highway 61 and Lake Superior. Be sure to stop on the downhill run before skidding out onto the highway.

FOR MORE INFORMATION
Split Rock Lighthouse State Park
2010A Highway 61 East
Two Harbors MN 55616
(218) 226-6377

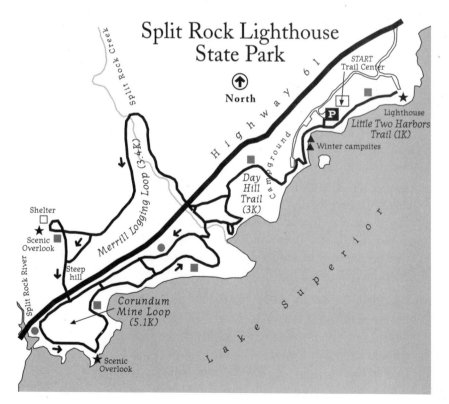

Split Rock Lighthouse State Park

Northwoods Ski Touring Trail

TRAILHEAD ACCESS
Take Outer Drive, which becomes Penn Blvd. and Forest Road 11, through the town of Silver Bay for a total of 3.2 miles from Highway 61 to signed parking area on right.

TOTAL TRAIL: 19K
Groomed Diagonal: 19K   Skating: none   Lit: none

PASS REQUIREMENTS
• Great Minnesota Ski Pass
• Recommended annual membership in club ($10/family, $5/individual, see address page 74) or use donation box at trailhead.

TRAILHEAD FACILITIES
None

SNOW CONDITIONS HOTLINE (218) 226-4334

WHAT MAKES IT UNIQUE
A "local" trail that adds a traditional twist to North Shore skiing. The narrow trails and great views make this feel like you are on the Superior Hiking Trail.

INTERPRETIVE FEATURE
Bean Lake is a favorite destination for hikers in the summer and skiers in the winter. It's one of the few lakes on North Shore ski trails, and is easily the most dramatic of these few, with its high walls seemingly dwarfing the lake itself.

MAPLE CORNER LOOPS (3.3K)

EASIER

These beginner loops quickly immerse you in the intimacy of this trail system as you climb gently along the banks of the east branch of the Beaver River. Be sure to sign in at the trail register...and check out the colorful comments of your fellow skiers. It's 2.8K around the outside loop and 2.1K around the inside loop. Use caution on the two snowmobile trail crossings. There are fun but easy downhill runs with terrific, mountainlike views.

BIG PINE CORNER LOOP (4.7K)

EASIER AND INTERMEDIATE

This trail weaves up the open country of the Beaver River and its tributary, Smokey Creek, to Big Pine Corner, crisscrossing a snowmobile trail then turning south. From there you can either huff it

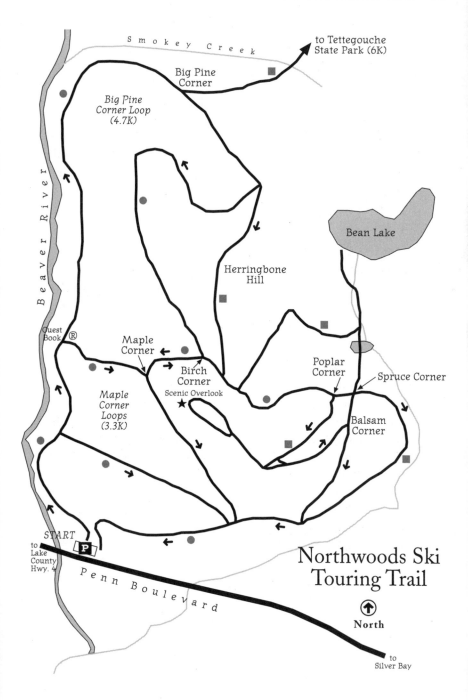

to Tettegouche
State Park (6K)

Smokey Creek

Big Pine
Corner

Big Pine
Corner Loop
(4.7K)

Bean Lake

Herringbone
Hill

Guest
Book ®

Maple
Corner

Birch
Corner
Scenic Overlook

Poplar
Corner

Spruce Corner

Maple
Corner
Loops
(3.3K)

Balsam
Corner

Beaver River

START
to
Lake
County
Hwy. 4

P

Penn Boulevard

Northwoods Ski
Touring Trail

⊕
North

to
Silver Bay

over Herringbone Hill, 0.9K of a big up and down, or continue on a level trail.

POPLAR/SPRUCE/BALSAM CORNERS (3.9K)

EASIER AND INTERMEDIATE

If you are an intermediate skier, put aside your agendas and take a loop or two through these hills in open woods. There are great views of the rugged hills to the north and east. The main trail is suitable for beginners. The side trails are intermediate: either climb up from Poplar Corner to the panoramic views from the scenic overlook or descend from Spruce Corner into the rolling hillside. The one-way trails feed you back to the trailhead where you can start over.

BEAN LAKE SPUR (1.1K)

INTERMEDIATE

Ski in either around or across (from Poplar Corner) a large beaver pond into the rugged territory of Bean Lake. Three different trails converge at the same place on the lake, so be careful on your way back that you choose the right one.

TETTEGOUCHE CONNECTOR (6K)

INTERMEDIATE

Although the terrain on this trail is relatively easy, because of the distance involved and the remoteness, this section should only be skied by experienced, prepared skiers. After crossing Smokey Creek, the trail follows the creek's upper reaches in a valley which gets narrower and narrower until you pass through a gorge with 250-foot sides. The trail crosses the Red Dot snowmobile trail twice on its way to Mic Mac Lake and Tettegouche Camp.

FOR MORE INFORMATION

Northwoods Ski Touring Club
Box 52
Silver Bay MN 55614
(218) 226-4334

Tettegouche State Park

TRAILHEAD ACCESS
Take Highway 61 four miles northeast of Silver Bay to park entrance. With a state park vehicle permit, head up park access road to parking lot at trailhead.

TOTAL TRAIL: 17.5K
Groomed Diagonal: 17.5K   Skating: 7.5K   Lit: none

PASS REQUIREMENTS
• Great Minnesota Ski Pass
• Minnesota State Parks vehicle permit

TRAILHEAD FACILITIES
Outhouses

WHAT MAKES IT UNIQUE
Long loops into quiet, dramatic country make for a real sense of adventure.

INTERPRETIVE FEATURE
The lower loop passes through one of the best stands of yellow birch on the North Shore. The yellow birch looks similar to paper birch except the bark is silvery-yellow and much more finely peeling. Another sure way to identify the yellow birch is to find a fresh twig and scratch the bark off: if it's a yellow birch, you will get a strong whiff of wintergreen. Unlike the paper birch, the yellow birch is a climax species and it can grow quite large and old: some of the biggest trees you will see along the shore are yellow birch. It is often found alongside the sugar maple.

LOWER LOOP (7.5K)

INTERMEDIATE / SKATING AND DIAGONAL

A classic North Shore ski outing, where you will climb through a nice variety of habitats then enjoy a thrilling downhill run back to the trailhead. Throw into the mix a nice inland lake, big old trees and almost 5K of skiing without an intersection to think about. The 2.9K climb to Nipisiquit Lake is nice enough, with a mix of younger forest and the opportunity to hack your way up to the Lake Superior overlook (this spur trail is not groomed). Nipisiquit Lake will take what's left of your breath away, and on a sunny afternoon the picnic spot there will tempt you to stay awhile. The trail back from Nipisiquit continues to climb past some wonderful yellow birch. Shortly after you cross the Superior Hiking Trail, on a fast day you will head downhill, with enough speed you will wish you had goggles.

LAKES AND HILLS (8.6K)

INTERMEDIATE AND ADVANCED

Watch for signs of wolf as you skirt the hills and lakeshores of this rugged terrain. After rounding Papasay Ridge ("Papasay stay on the trail!"), you will be back on Nipisiquit Lake. This may tempt you to ski across the ice on your way back, but do so only with extreme caution, especially near the streams that empty out of or into the lake. Mic Mac and Tettegouche Lakes are next. If you haven't made your reservation at the cabins on Mic Mac, you will want to do so for next year once you see them. The trail in from the parking lot on Lax Lake Road is actually a road, but is steep enough to keep its intermediate ranking. Advanced skiers only can take a run on the 2.6K Mount Baldy trail.

Lake-effect snow

Want huge amounts of fresh, fluffy snow? Then hope for a southeast wind. Although rare, the southeast wind draws moisture from the open lake. When that moist air reaches land, the cold of the land mass and the height of the hills draw out the moisture—and it snows like crazy, especially along the ridgeline. So-called "lake-effect snow" can dump up to five feet of snow, as it did in 1994 in the Silver Bay-Finland area. ❄

TETTEGOUCHE CONNECTOR

See entry for the Northwoods Ski Touring Trail (page 74).

ASSOCIATED LODGING

Tettegouche Camp offers rustic, ski-in only lodging in four log cabins. Reservations are available up to one year in advance. Call (800) 246-2267.

FOR MORE INFORMATION

Tettegouche State Park
474 Highway 61 East
Silver Bay MN 55614
(218) 226-6365

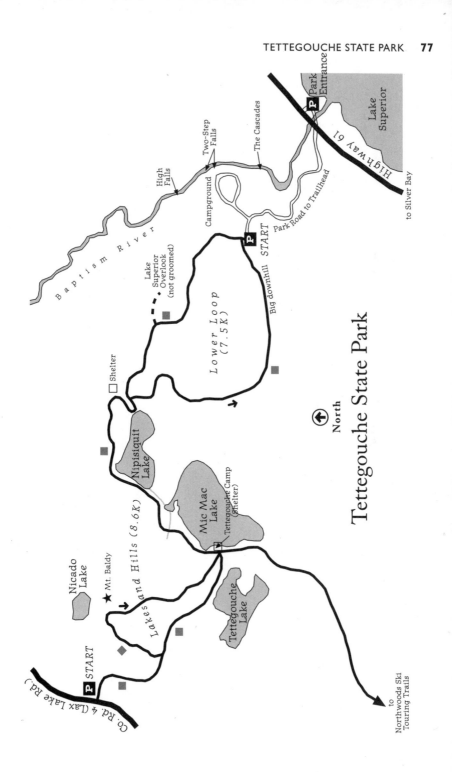

Tettegouche State Park

Finland Ski Trail

TRAILHEAD ACCESS
Take County Road 7 (Cramer Road) one mile east of Finland to
parking area on right, just past Recreation Center.

TOTAL TRAIL: 5K
Groomed Diagonal: 5K   Skating: none   Lit: none

PASS REQUIREMENTS
• Great Minnesota Ski Pass

TRAILHEAD FACILITIES
None

WHAT MAKES IT UNIQUE
Challenging, out-of-the way trails provide solitude and
excitement.

INTERPRETIVE FEATURE
The infant Baptism River runs along the northern edge of a large
intrusion of gabbro, part of what is known as the Beaver Bay
Complex. When you cross the river (which runs on top of softer
volcanic rock) and begin climbing, it is up the ridge created by
the erosion-resistant gabbro.

FIRST LOOP (3.5K)

INTERMEDIATE TO ADVANCED

After a level 0.6K on the access trail in the meadows along the
intimate East Branch of the Baptism River, you will cross the
Baptism and enter a dark forest. You'll soon learn why this narrow
trail is for intermediate to advanced skiers, as you climb 80 feet
right away along a winding trail, and then another 110 feet to a
lookout. The higher you go, the more maple trees you will find.
The run back on the other side of the loop is equally winding, past
a rocky bluff.

SECOND LOOP (1.5K)

INTERMEDIATE TO ADVANCED

As long as you are up on the ridge, stay up high in the maples. The
second loop starts out level, then climbs 50 more feet into rugged
country before descending and rejoining the first loop below the
bluff.

Future trails may also be developed to the south and east of the
existing loops, so keep an eye out!

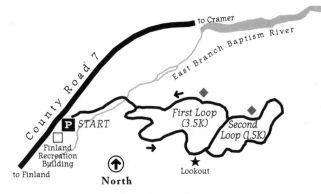

Finland Ski Trail

FOR MORE INFORMATION
Gary Nelson
39 Park Hill Road
Finland MN 55603
(218) 353-7521

Flathorn-Gegoka

TRAILHEAD ACCESS
Take Highway 1 seven miles west of Isabella either to Lake Gegoka Boat Landing or National Forest Lodge.

TOTAL TRAIL: 30.6K
Groomed Diagonal: 30.6K   Skating: none   Lit: none

PASS REQUIREMENTS
• Great Minnesota Ski Pass

TRAILHEAD FACILITIES
None at boat landing. Full services at National Forest Lodge, available only to registered guests.

WHAT MAKES IT UNIQUE
Many white pines and lakes give this a real "Boundary Waters" feel.

INTERPRETIVE FEATURE
The beautiful white pine forest here is the result of humans and nature working together. Although the pine forest appears primordial, it has been aggressively managed. Selective cutting has allowed the strongest pines to grow even bigger and stronger.

CENTRAL LOOPS (10K)

EASIEST

These loops offer tremendous variety among the big pines on a combination of old logging roads and forest roads. The connector routes provide beautiful skiing through black spruce bogs and cedar swamps.

EASTERN LOOPS (7.4K)

INTERMEDIATE

These more challenging trails lead the skier around Flathorn Lake, in the area that was once the Environmental Learning Center. Two crossings of the Isabella River are especially pretty as the river flows all year long.

NORTHERN LOOPS (10.2K)

INTERMEDIATE

Move out of the white pine into the realm of red pine, Minnesota's state tree. Spruce bogs complete the coniferous diversity. A shelter at intersection twenty-six is a good lunch destination for a day-long outing on the northern loops.

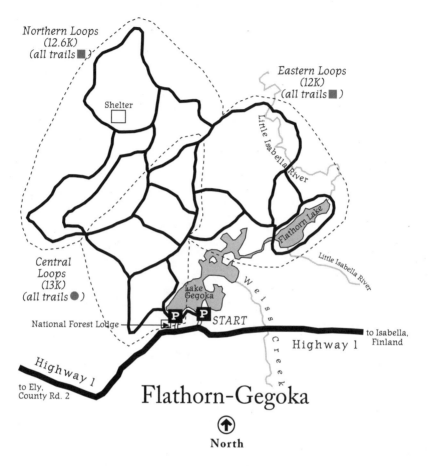

Flathorn-Gegoka

North

ASSOCIATED LODGING
National Forest Lodge

FOR MORE INFORMATION
National Forest Lodge
3226 Highway 1
Isabella MN 55607
(218) 323-7676

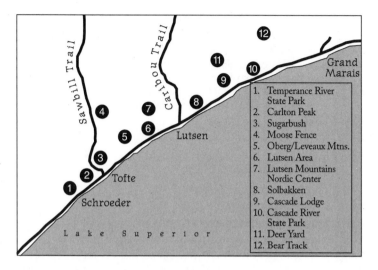

1. Temperance River State Park
2. Carlton Peak
3. Sugarbush
4. Moose Fence
5. Oberg/Leveaux Mtns.
6. Lutsen Area
7. Lutsen Mountains Nordic Center
8. Solbakken
9. Cascade Lodge
10. Cascade River State Park
11. Deer Yard
12. Bear Track

North Shore Mountains
Cross-Country Ski Trails

Have you ever put on your skis and had such a good time you didn't want to stop? Here you don't have to. Over 200K of interconnected trails await, linking the Temperance River to Bear Track trails, nearly to Grand Marais. The well-maintained trails weave in and out of the Sawtooth Mountains, connecting to tony lodges and B&Bs along the way. From Carlton Peak to the Cascade River the trails are groomed ten to fifteen feet wide by Pisten-Bully groomers. At the far ends, the more rustic trails of Temperance, Cascade River State Park and Bear Track await. While backcountry adventurers head out on the 25K Picnic Loop, families cruise the Cascade River trails. If all you want to do is zoom downhill, arrange a shuttle for a long glide back to the lake, or check out Lutsen Mountain's "norpine" trails. Don't stop 'till you get to the espresso!

Temperance River State Park

TRAILHEAD ACCESS
There are two trailheads: (1) Take the Skou Road directly across Highway 61 from Schroeder gas station (milepost 79.1) 0.2 miles to trailhead; (2) Temperance River State Park at the parking areas on Highway 61 on the west side of river.

TOTAL TRAIL: 12.6K
Groomed Diagonal: 12.6K   Skating: none   Lit: none

PASS REQUIREMENTS
• Great Minnesota Ski Pass

TRAILHEAD FACILITIES
None

SNOWPHONE (800) 897-7669

WHAT MAKES IT UNIQUE
Shelters along the trails make this perfect for a picnic outing, especially on days when a little break from the wind is welcome. These trails are groomed six feet wide with a single track for diagonal skiing.

INTERPRETIVE FEATURE
While Temperance River is known by most park visitors as a roaring cascade out of sight in a dark, deep gorge, the winter visitor can see the other side of the river's personality—a gentle, meandering stream, perhaps resting before it plummets through the canyon. This split personality is typical of North Shore streams: long sections of relatively gentle flow along glacial outwash, followed by a wild rush as the river cuts through a layer of bedrock.

Trail status is changing year to year. Check in at Temperance River State Park office for a current map.

CROSS RIVER LOOPS (6.7K)

EASIER TO INTERMEDIATE

Depending on how you navigate these trails, you can make a number of different loops of around 3K each. The trickiest part of any of these loops will be right along the Cross River, where some steep hills await. Otherwise you are cruising through mixed deciduous woods with scattered glens of spruce. Three shelters are scattered around; the upper one has a nice view of the Cross River valley and even includes an outhouse.

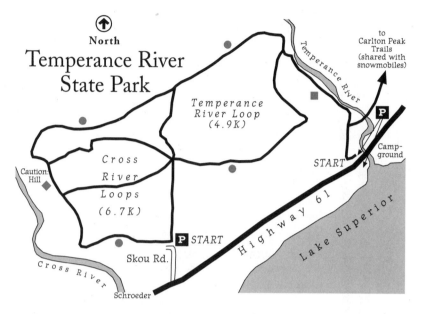

TEMPERANCE RIVER LOOP (4.9K)

INTERMEDIATE

This loop is contiguous with the Cross River Loops but can also be skied easily from the state park end. To do so, take the almost 1K of trail which follows the Temperance River bank before climbing out to the unplowed road. From here it's a 3.6K complete clockwise loop or you can end by skiing down the road and walking back to the trailhead.

FOR MORE INFORMATION
Temperance River State Park
PO Box 33
Schroeder MN 55613
(218) 663-7476

Carlton Peak

TRAILHEAD ACCESS
There are two trailheads: (1) For the Britton Peak/Sugarbush trailhead, take Sawbill Trail 2.7 miles north of Highway 61; (2) For the Tofte trailhead, go directly uphill from the main entrance of Bluefin Bay Resort.

TOTAL TRAIL: 9K
Groomed Diagonal: 9K   Skating: 9K   Lit: none

PASS REQUIREMENTS
• Great Minnesota Ski Pass

TRAILHEAD FACILITIES
Full services in Tofte. Outhouse at Sugarbush.

SNOWPHONE (800) 897-7669

WHAT MAKES IT UNIQUE
Tremendous views of, and possibly from, Carlton Peak.

INTERPRETIVE FEATURE
Carlton Peak is officially one of the highest "mountains" in Minnesota when measured from its base to its summit. The peak is composed of two large chunks of anorthosite, a highly erosion-resistant rock. The quarry visible on the southeast side of the mountain provided rock for the breakwater at Taconite Harbor. Until 1993 the peak was owned by 3M Company, which had hoped to mine abrasive metals. Instead, 3M contributed the land to Temperance River State Park.

SUMMIT VIEW (2.2K)
INTERMEDIATE

Follow this summertime road up to the shoulder of Carlton Peak. The trail initially takes you through mostly open country before leading you to the base of the peak. From here you could change to snowshoes and hop on the Superior Hiking Trail to the summit, but watch out: one wrong move and even the deepest snow won't catch your fall.

BLUEFIN TRAIL (3K)
INTERMEDIATE

This trail is best used for so-called "norpine" skiing. Get someone to drive you to the Britton Peak trailhead, then ski downhill back to the lake and the Bluefin Bay trailhead. This is a fun run through a mostly birch forest. Be sure to look off to your right in some of

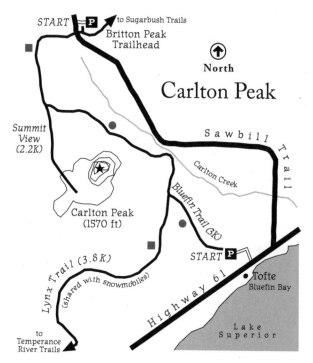

the open areas for a dramatic view of Carlton Peak and the quarry on its southeast "face."

LYNX TRAIL (3.8K)
EASIER

Although officially part of the interconnecting North Shore Mountains trail system, this link to Temperance River State Park has returned to its origins as a popular snowmobile trail and is no longer groomed for skiing. To make the connection with Temperance you can still ski this, but remember you are a guest—if a snowmobile comes along, ski off to the side and let it pass.

FOR MORE INFORMATION
Lutsen Tofte Tourism Association
Box 2248, Tofte MN 55615 (218) 663-7804

Dogsledding outfitters
Up and down the shore you will find local mushers eager to take you and your family out for a ride with their dogs. You can go for an hour, a day, even overnight or for a week! The people providing these services change from year to year, so your best bet is to contact the local chamber of commerce or tourism association for names. ✳

Sugarbush

TRAILHEAD ACCESS
Take Sawbill Trail 2.7 miles north of Tofte and Highway 61 to
Britton Peak trailhead on right, with large parking area at
trailhead.

TOTAL TRAIL: 44K
Groomed Diagonal: 44K   Skating: 44K   Lit: none

PASS REQUIREMENTS
• Great Minnesota Ski Pass

TRAILHEAD FACILITIES
Outhouse

SNOWPHONE (800) 897-7669

WHAT MAKES IT UNIQUE
Excellent trails, easy access and proximity to resorts make this
area a popular starting point for a North Shore ski vacation.
The Picnic Loop is one of the most challenging ski outings in
the area. Since these trails are heavily used, grooming is frequent.

INTERPRETIVE FEATURE
The maple trees which dominate this area are common along
ridgelines from Duluth to Grand Marais and in scattered areas in
Grand Portage and even Thunder Bay. Watch on these trails as
you climb into maple-rich highlands and then zoom down into
lower areas where birch, spruce and cedar replace the maple.

INNER LOOPS (2.9K)

EASIER

Entering the magnificent Sugarbush trails, these first loops are
great for warm-ups or for introducing novices to the basics. Ag-
gressive skiers will speed through these loops, but it's worth taking
a few minutes to enjoy the views through the maples of Carlton
Peak. Wood Duck Loop is named for a small pond it passes with
a wood duck nesting box. The north sides of the loops are groomed
wider for better skate skiing. True beginners should be a little careful
on the north part of the first loop as it enters the parking lot:
without good braking or a turn, you could end up in the road.

HOGBACK LOOP (3.1K)

INTERMEDIATE

If you are ready for a little more challenge, take the long climb up
from the Piece of Cake Loop onto Hogback Ridge. You'll quickly

leave behind the crowds and enjoy some challenging hills. The first half of the clockwise loop follows the Superior National Forest boundary, as marked by the yellow signs. There's one last climb after the junction with the Picnic Loop, then a long, gradual downhill to the end of the loop.

BRIDGE RUN LOOP (1.7K)
INTERMEDIATE

This is a nice introduction to intermediate skiing, with a fast but straight downhill to kick off the loop (this is the two-way ski-through trail, so watch out for people coming the other way). The herringbone climb back up to the Piece of Cake Loop is challenging—but you will have more fun continuing on to the Homestead Loop.

HOMESTEAD LOOP (7.3K)
INTERMEDIATE

This makes a great half-day outing. As a counterclockwise loop it saves the best for last: a 4.5K run through the maples with no stops or intersections, just a gradual climb, great views of the Sawtooth mountains both up and down the shore, and two or three fun, short downhills to finish. The best lunch stop is about three quarters of the way along the southern section, with a southern-facing overlook of Leveaux Mountain. Starting and ending at the Sawbill Trail, this makes for about a 12K ski.

Anomalous maples and snowbound spruce

The sugar maple and yellow birch are trees of the northern hardwood forest. Given its latitude, the North Shore should be too far north for this sort of forest. Anywhere the temperature drops below about -45°F, sugar maple and yellow birch cannot survive. The North Shore ought to be a boreal forest of spruce, birch and pine, except for one important factor: the warming influence of Lake Superior. On the ridgelines where these maples grow, the warm lake keeps the temperature from dropping below that killing point of -45°F even on the coldest night.

In the valleys of the North Shore highlands, the forest is more like it "should" be for this latitude. Spruce, birch and alder dominate. These are frost pockets, where the cold air that sinks off the ridgeline accumulates and, cut off from the heat of the lake, drops the temperature to ranges inhospitable to the yellow birch and sugar maple.

Broadly speaking, the ridges are like a forest from Central Minnesota while the valleys come from Northern Ontario. The combination of these habitats is nothing less than spectacular. ❄

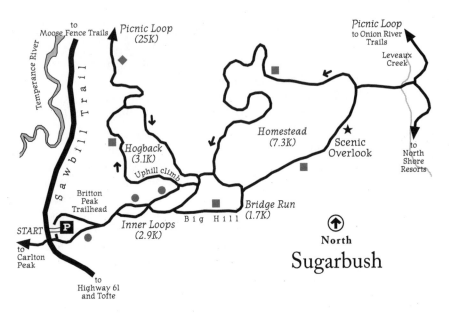

PICNIC LOOP (25K)
INTERMEDIATE AND ADVANCED
This is the classic North Shore ski adventure. The Picnic Loop is an annual ritual for many, a chance to immerse in the woods for an entire day while experiencing remote country on challenging trails. The loop incorporates parts of the Hogback and Homestead loops, as well as the Sixmile Crossing Trail that starts at the Moose Fence trailhead. The low parts of the trail have some cedar, while on high ground it's more maple forest. The downhill run after the junction with Sixmile Crossing Trail is an exciting set of switchbacks.

LEVEAUX MOUNTAIN TRAILS (4K)
INTERMEDIATE
These trails connect the Picnic Loop and the North Shore Mountains ski-through trail with resorts on the shore, including the Cliff Dweller, Cobblestone Cabins and Chateau Leveaux. They are not always groomed. If you are staying at one of the connecting resorts, ask about conditions before heading out.

FOR MORE INFORMATION
Lutsen Tofte Tourism Association
Box 2248, Tofte MN 55615 (218) 663-7804

Moose Fence

TRAILHEAD ACCESS
Take the Sawbill Trail 7.5 miles north of Highway 61 to small, signed parking lot on right directly off road.

TOTAL TRAIL: 9K
Groomed Diagonal: 9K   Skating: 9K   Lit: none

PASS REQUIREMENTS
• Great Minnesota Ski Pass

TRAILHEAD FACILITIES
None

SNOWPHONE (800) 897-7669

WHAT MAKES IT UNIQUE
These trails are at 1450 feet and over five miles away from Lake Superior, so they have a longer season than the other Sugarbush-area trails. They are also the most family-friendly of the Sugarbush-area trails, with wide tracks, easy terrain and fewer people.

INTERPRETIVE FEATURE
The name of this area tells all sorts of stories. When the trails were first developed, there was a fence built to keep moose out of a ten acre plot of experimental white pine. The young white pine were part of an experiment to breed trees resistant to white pine blister rust, a disease which kills many white pine before they can reach maturity. The fence is gone now, but a healthy stand of white pine remains.

MAPLE LOOP (3.4K)

EASIER

A 0.9K access trail takes you from the trailhead up over a small ridge to the beginning of this loop. The hill down to the start of the loop is the biggest on the whole route. As the name implies, there is a lot of maple here, but also some nice open glades. Take the loop counterclockwise; the south side is a little hillier than the north, and you will climb about 150 feet, but none of it is steep.

UPLAND LOOP (2.4K)

EASIER

This is what is known as a "lollipop loop." The "stick" of the lollipop is the 0.4K two-way trail at the beginning. And the "candy" part of the lollipop really is sweet: almost 2K of level, open skiing on top of an easy ridge. Chances are you will want to ski this loop

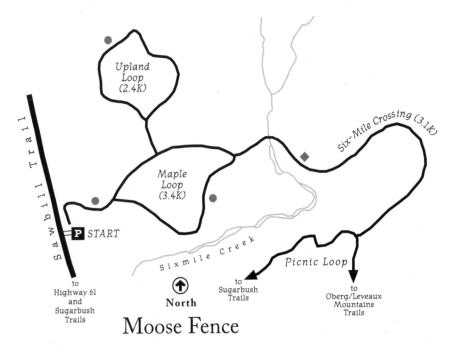

Upland
Loop
(2.4K)

Sawbill Trail

Six-Mile Crossing (3.1K)

Maple
Loop
(3.4K)

P START

Sixmile Creek

Picnic Loop

to
Highway 61
and
Sugarbush
Trails

to
Sugarbush
Trails

to
Oberg/Leveaux
Mountains
Trails

⊕
North

Moose Fence

twice before heading back. Wildlife signs are common, including deer and a variety of birds.

SIXMILE CROSSING (3.1K)

ADVANCED

This section of trail connects Moose Fence with the Picnic Loop and the main Sugarbush region. It provides an opportunity for "norpine" skiing from the Moose Fence Trailhead down to the Onion River/Oberg Mountain trailhead, though with a little more work than other norpine routes—the climb out of the valley of Sixmile Creek is pretty steep. Notice the boreal spruce forest in the Sixmile Creek valley: cold air sinks from the maple ridges and keeps out the "riff-raff"—trees that can't survive temperatures below -40°.

FOR MORE INFORMATION

Lutsen Tofte Tourism Association
Box 2248
Tofte MN 55615
(218) 663-7804

Oberg/Leveaux Mountains

TRAILHEAD ACCESS
Take Onion River Road (Forest Road 336) 2.1 miles north of
Highway 61 to large parking area on left where plowed road
ends.

TOTAL TRAIL: 19K
Groomed Diagonal: 19K   Skating: 19K   Lit: none

PASS REQUIREMENTS
• Great Minnesota Ski Pass

TRAILHEAD FACILITIES
Outhouse

SNOWPHONE (800) 897-7669

WHAT MAKES IT UNIQUE
Views of Leveaux Peak are dramatic, while the Onion River Road
provides ideal skate skiing terrain.

INTERPRETIVE FEATURE
The rock that tops off Leveaux Mountain and provides its
dramatic appearance comes from a major intrusion of basaltic
lava. This same formation is found on top of Eagle Mountain at
Lutsen and may be the same rock at Pincushion Mountain near
Grand Marais. One 36-mile long chunk of lava is responsible for
some of the best skiing terrain along the North Shore.

OBERG MOUNTAIN TRAIL (8.1K)

INTERMEDIATE

This is a classic climb up into maple forest, with added views of
Oberg Lake. After a long climb you will be rewarded with a relatively long level stretch through the thick maples before a quick
descent back to the Onion River Road. You can return to the
trailhead by the road, but the views along the ski trail are much
better, with Leveaux rising out of open fields like a scene from the
mountains of Montana.

ONION RIVER ROAD (4K)

EASIER / SKATING

This is one of the few parts of the public North Shore Mountains
system that's managed specifically for skate skiing. The trail is actually the continuation of Onion River Road (Forest Road 336),
and is groomed nearly wide enough for side-by-side skate skiing.
The level to rolling terrain makes this ideal for instruction. Late

season skiers will find snow here longer than other sections: in 1996, locals were still skiing this stretch on May 7.

LUTSEN CONNECTORS / ROLLINS CREEK (7K)
INTERMEDIATE
From where they leave the Oberg Mountain Trail 1.4K from the parking lot on Onion River Road, these trails lead either 2.6K downhill to the Lutsen Sea Villas or 5K to the Superior National Golf Course. In both cases, the trails are not always groomed, so pick your way carefully.

FOR MORE INFORMATION
Lutsen Tofte Tourism Association
Box 2248, Tofte MN 55615
(218) 663-7804

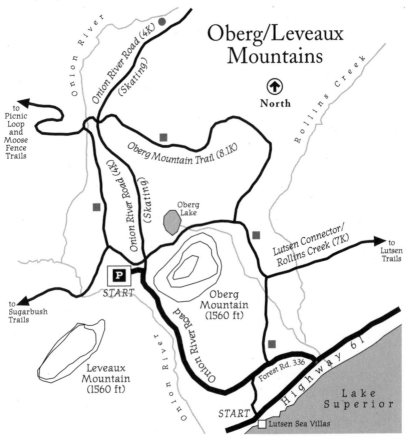

Lutsen Area

TRAILHEAD ACCESS
There are three trailhead locations: (1) Take entrance road to Superior National golf course clubhouse either to clubhouse or to the maintenance shed; (2) Take County Road 36 about 1.5 miles from Highway 61 to the stables and park by the gate; (3) Take Caribou Trail 1.4 miles up from Highway 61 to small parking lot on left.

TOTAL TRAIL: 7K
Groomed Diagonal: 7K   Skating: 7K   Lit: none

PASS REQUIREMENTS
• Great Minnesota Ski Pass

TRAILHEAD FACILITIES
None

SNOWPHONE (800) 897-7669

WHAT MAKES IT UNIQUE
There are great plans for this location. The potential for night skiing on the Golf Course Loop, in combination with interpretive programs at the clubhouse, could make for a great northwoods evening out. For the present, however, this is mostly just a link in the North Shore Mountains system between the Sugarbush and Solbakken trails and a quick outing for guests of Lutsen Resort.

INTERPRETIVE FEATURE
East of County Road 36, the trail crosses through the Lutsen Scientific and Natural Area. This is one of the largest areas of old growth northern hardwood forest on the North Shore, with some trees ranging in age from 145 to 300 years old. It is the only known regional habitat of the *moschatel,* a delicate little wildflower that is typically only found in forests much further south. You won't see it in winter, but it's awfully nice to know that it's there.

HOMESTEAD ACRES (5K)

INTERMEDIATE

This is a connector trail between the Lutsen area and the Solbakken trails. From the golf course trailhead, it crosses the Poplar River and County Road 36. A spur trail comes down from the Lutsen stables, where parking is available. The trail cuts through the Lutsen Scientific and Natural Area, with some spectacular old-growth hardwoods. Watch out for snowmobile trail crossings, as you may encounter them in the middle of a downhill run.

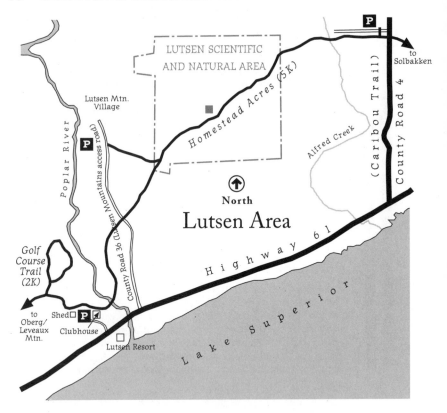

GOLF COURSE TRAIL (APPX. 2K)

EASIER

This trail starts either from the Superior National golf course club house or the maintenance shed a few hundred yards farther in past the parking lot. It's a two-way trail with a stem (which meets the trail connecting to the Oberg/Leveaux trails) and a loop of about 1.5K. The route of the loop changes during the winter depending on grooming and snow conditions. Since this trail follows open golf course terrain, the track is susceptible to windblown snow. Still, it's a nice, sunny option for guests of Lutsen Resort.

FOR MORE INFORMATION

Lutsen Tofte Tourism Association
Box 2248
Tofte MN 55615
(218) 663-7804

Lutsen Mountains Nordic Center

TRAILHEAD ACCESS
Take County Road 36 2.8 miles north of Highway 61 to Lutsen Mountain. Park as near the main chalet as you can, as that's where tickets are sold. If possible, park in the upper lot to be close to the trailhead and tickets.

TOTAL TRAIL: 31K
Groomed Diagonal: 31K   Skating: 31K   Lit: none

PASS REQUIREMENTS
• Day passes available at main chalet ($12/adult, $6/children).

TRAILHEAD FACILITIES
Full services including food and ski rental.

WHAT MAKES IT UNIQUE
This is the only "private" ski area in this part of the North Shore, which should ensure a higher level of maintenance and care. The emphasis is on "norpine" skiing, with chairlifts taking you to higher elevations and allowing you to ski mostly downhill.

INTERPRETIVE FEATURE
Moose Mountain is a classic "sawtooth" formation within the Sawtooth Mountains. The side facing Lake Superior is a gradual rise representing the tilted top of a large lava flow. The north-western side is a sharp drop, representing the edge of the lava flows like the edge of a broken plate.

The following loops are designed to be taken in the outlined order. These trails are not well-suited for beginners, due to the constant downhill runs, use of chairlifts and sharp turns.

ULLR MOUNTAIN (5K)

EASIEST

This is the typical start for a day of lifts and loops. Take the Ullr Mountain chairlift and head straight into the woods from the top of the lift. Within moments you will leave behind the neon rush of the downhill slopes and enter a quiet maple forest for the first half of the downhill run. In the last half of the trail you will over-look the scenic Poplar River valley. If 5K is all you want to do, head back to the trailhead. Otherwise, double back at the 'Y' in-tersection for the Mystery Mountain trails. Although this is labelled "easiest," it requires good control on some relatively tight downhill turns.

LOWER MYSTERY MOUNTAIN (9K)
MORE DIFFICULT

This is the next recommended section on the tour. You'll cross the Poplar River and pass an old cabin in a field with a scenic view of Lutsen's Eagle Mountain. After 1K you will cross under the Mystery Mountain chair. Continue downhill underneath the lift and across the runs of the recently reopened Mystery Mountain. There are some particularly sharp turns in this section, so be prepared. At the base, you can take the Mystery Mountain chairlift and either loop back and forth across the downhill runs or head into the backcountry for Upper and Middle Mystery.

Lutsen Resort

The town of Lutsen is named after Lützen, a village in Germany where the Swedish king Gustavus Adolphus II was killed in a 1632 battle. The only battle you will find in this Lutsen is for the best parking spaces as the North Shore's most popular tourist destination rolls out its winter offerings. It wasn't nearly so crazy at the turn of the century when Carl Axel Nelson first started hosting moose hunters. That was the start of a long tradition of hospitality. Today Lutsen Mountain and Lutsen Resort, in the classic lakeshore lodge, are separate businesses. But together they provide a dynamic and far-reaching North Shore winter destination. ✳

UPPER AND MIDDLE MYSTERY MOUNTAIN (10K)
MORE DIFFICULT

After a chairlift ride, you can continue your quiet ski trip further up the ridge of Mystery Mountain to the back side. Upper Mystery leads down the north side of the ridge in a winding 5K downhill run that will take you past another old cabin that's worth a stop and look. This route takes you back to the Mystery chairlift. Middle Mystery starts at a junction on the ridgetop 1.6K into Upper Mystery and leads 5K down the south side of the ridge to the Moose Mountain chairlift, leading you to the next stage.

MOOSE MOUNTAIN (7K)
MOST DIFFICULT

From the Mountain Top Deli, enjoy a relatively easy trip (7K round trip) along the ridgeline of Moose Mountain. Partway back you can take a 3.4K downhill run traversing around the base of the ski runs. Watch out for downhillers here! To return to the start, ride the chairlift to the top of the gondola and take the gondola down. Although this is labelled "most difficult," much of the trail is easy going, especially along the ridgeline.

ASSOCIATED LODGING
Numerous Lutsen Mountains lodging options directly on or nearby ski trails. Call (800) 360-7666.

FOR MORE INFORMATION
Lutsen Mountains Nordic Center
PO Box 129, Lutsen MN 55612 (218) 663-7281

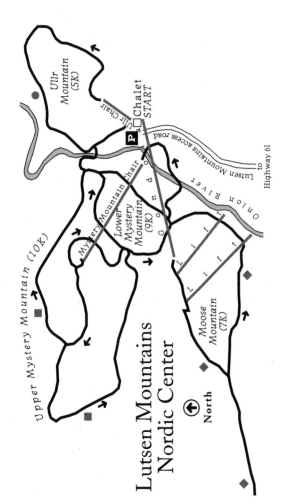

Solbakken

TRAILHEAD ACCESS
There are two trailheads: (1) Take County Road 41 (Hall Road) 0.4 miles up from Highway 61 to small parking lot on left; (2) Park at Solbakken's Resort on Highway 61, milepost 94. There is also a small parking lot at the trailhead directly off Highway 61 across from Solbakken's.

TOTAL TRAIL: 25K
Groomed Diagonal: 25K   Skating: 25K   Lit: none

PASS REQUIREMENTS
• Great Minnesota Ski Pass

TRAILHEAD FACILITIES
Full services at Solbakken including rental, instruction and dining. No services on Hall Road.

SNOWPHONE (800) 897-7669

WHAT MAKES IT UNIQUE
The history of homesteading on the North Shore comes alive in these loops named after the original settlers.

INTERPRETIVE FEATURE
The two western loops, Massie Loop and Isak's Flats, take you past virtually every sort of deciduous tree—trees that drop their leaves in the fall—found on the North Shore. You'll find every kind of northwoods deciduous tree except the sugar maple. There's even a stand of the deciduous conifer, the tamarack. The advantage of dropping leaves in the fall are many: it's virtually impossible to keep a broad green leaf from freezing and dying, wide leaves catch snow which could break limbs from the weight, and dead leaves on the ground add to soil fertility.

WHITESIDES / DEER TRACK LOOPS (2.1K)
EASIER AND INTERMEDIATE
The first of these two short loops is the 0.8K Deer Track Loop, named for the deer which frequent the plentiful cedar here. This is nice and flat for beginners. Whitesides Loop is a little hillier as it runs along Jonvik Creek

ISAK'S FLATS LOOP (2.3K)
EASIER
This is a recent addition to the Solbakken system which climbs gradually through a mixed deciduous forest and returns through a field of the old Massie homestead. There is a lot of ash on this loop, indicating that if you were here in summer you'd get your feet wet.

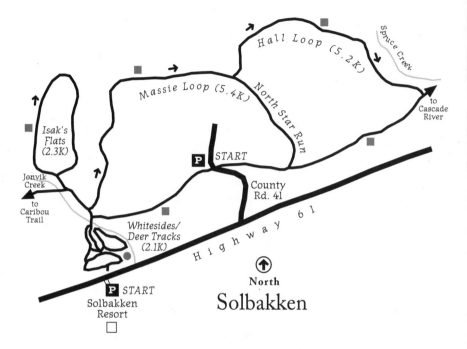

CARIBOU TRAIL CONNECTOR (1.8K)

INTERMEDIATE

This trail presents an easy opportunity for "norpine" skiing from the trailhead on the Caribou Trail about 450 vertical feet back down to Solbakken. Unlike the other trails here, this has two double tracks so you can ski side-by-side up before zooming back down again.

MASSIE LOOP (5.4K)

INTERMEDIATE

After climbing through an open area and passing the abandoned Massie homestead, enjoy a magical run through a thick grove of cedar. The downhill run of the North Star run is the only *official* big downhill on the whole western side. *Unofficially* there is the unmaintained downhill on the east side of Jonvik Creek named by a ski writer as Suicide Hill, which allows you to ski directly back to Solbakken Resort without passing through the Whitesides and Deer Track trails.

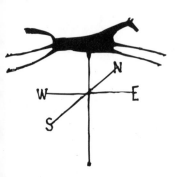

Weather patterns

If you don't like the weather, wait fifteen minutes. That old expression doesn't really work here. The weather in this region changes on cycles of 3–4 days. That means if you are just here for a short weekend, you might not see much change. If you spend a week on the North Shore, you will see whole weather systems moving in and out. Grey, 20 degree days turn into snowy days, followed by northwest winds bringing frigid air from the arctic. And then it starts all over again.

❄

HALL LOOP (5.2K)
INTERMEDIATE

Continue from the top of the Massie Loop on the Hall Loop, named after the other family to homestead this area. In contrast with the Massie Loop, this is mostly evergreen trees, including scenic glades of young spruce. Like the Massie Loop, the southern part of this loop is open forest, with plenty of openings for wildlife: watch for plentiful deer sign and the possible wolf sign that follows.

SPRUCE CREEK CONNECTOR TRAIL (8.5K)

The through-skier or those who have a way to shuttle will enjoy this section connecting Solbakken and the Cascade trails.

ASSOCIATED LODGING

Solbakken Resort offers full-service lodging immediately adjacent to these trails.

FOR MORE INFORMATION

Solbakken Resort
4874 W. Highway 61
Lutsen MN 55612
(218) 663-7566 or (800) 435-3950
solbakken@boreal.org

Cascade River State Park

TRAILHEAD ACCESS
There are two trailheads: (1) Enter Cascade River State Park at
milepost 100 on Highway 61 and take park road to Trail Center;
(2) Use small parking lot at milepost 98 with access to trails on
west side of river.

TOTAL TRAIL: 12.5K
Groomed Diagonal: 12.5K   Skating: none   Lit: none

PASS REQUIREMENTS
• Great Minnesota Ski Pass
• Minnesota State Park vehicle permit

TRAILHEAD FACILITIES
Bathrooms

SNOWPHONE (800) 897-7669

WHAT MAKES IT UNIQUE
This park provides the only opportunity in the North Shore
Mountains system as well as in all of Cook County for Lake
Superior lakeshore skiing. But this opportunity doesn't always
last long; when there is fresh snow, get out there and do it! Trails
are groomed only six feet wide, so you'll feel close to the diverse
forest.

INTERPRETIVE FEATURE
The cedar woods here are a wonderful winter habitat for both
humans and the white-tailed deer. The trees provide shelter from
the wind, low snow depth, and most importantly, a delicious
food (for an animal with four stomachs!). The deer eat the
succulent greenery as high up on the tree as they can reach,
creating neatly trimmed bases.

SHORELINE LOOP (2.8K)

EASIEST AND MORE DIFFICULT

This is your only opportunity in Cook County and the North Shore
Mountains system to ski right along the shore of Lake Superior.
After dropping down through the (closed) campground and a careful crossing of Highway 61, enjoy a mostly-flat run just a few yards
from the waves or the ice. The track may be a little rough right on
the highway due to sun exposure, so be careful. Snow conditions
must be optimal for good skiing on this loop.

White-tailed deer

Some of the most obvious wildlife signs you will see in winter are those of the white-tailed deer. This animal is tough. Because their narrow hooves don't ride above the snow, deer develop and maintain a network of packed trails through their choice winter habitat of cedar groves. Their four stomachs allow them to browse on everything from grass to tree bark, the stomachs progressively turning rough plant material into essential nutrients. ❄

CEDAR WOODS (6.4K)
EASIEST TO ADVANCED

This is a great cruise through cedar woods with lots of deer sign. Skiing clockwise you can make this all a beginner's loop, starting on the river ridge trails. Otherwise, you can climb gradually in a counterclockwise direction, then enjoy either one of two intermediate downhills or a wild advanced downhill (dropping 200 feet in 0.6K). The trails along the edge of the Cascade River Valley offer dramatic views of the valley and Lookout Mountain, set in pines.

The trail across the Cascade River is quite tricky on skis, and since you don't want to lose control so close to the gorge of a rushing river, you'd be best served by taking off your skis and walking.

MOOSE MOUNTAIN (3.2K)
INTERMEDIATE TO ADVANCED

Depart from the cedar woods and climb another 220 feet to the shelter on top of Moose Mountain. The last section of trail is a real challenge, but the view of Lake Superior is worth it.

BALLY CREEK CONNECTOR (10K)

See entry for Bear Track (page 111).

FOR MORE INFORMATION

Cascade River State Park
3481 W. Highway 61
Lutsen MN 55612
(218) 387-3053

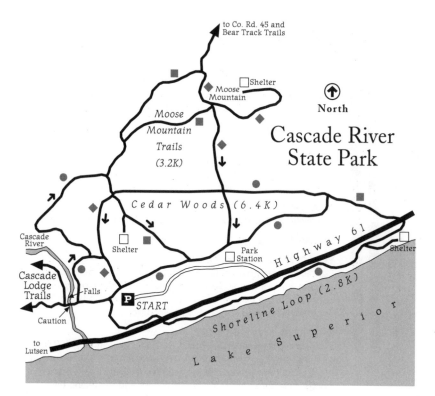

Deer and wolf population

The population of white-tailed deer on the North Shore represents a delicate balance. In winter, the number of deer close to the shore increases greatly as outsiders move in for Lake Superior's warmer climate and less-deep snow. This increased density of deer makes for an increase in car-deer accidents; driving carefully to your trailhead helps both you and the deer. More deer has also meant more wolves in an area with relatively well-developed commercial facilities. So watch for tracks and keep your pets on a leash. ❄

Cascade Lodge

TRAILHEAD ACCESS
Cascade Lodge is at Highway 61 milepost 99, ten miles southwest of Grand Marais. Reach the trailhead at the top of the road
that leads through the resort, past the cabins.

TOTAL TRAIL: 14.4K
Groomed Diagonal: 14.4K   Skating: 1.5K   Lit: none

PASS REQUIREMENTS
• Great Minnesota Ski Pass
• Other fees: $3.50/day parking for non-guests; maps $1

TRAILHEAD FACILITIES
Full facilities at Cascade Lodge including ski rental and dining.

SNOWPHONE (800) 260-SNOW

WHAT MAKES IT UNIQUE
Cascade Lodge provides true ski-from-your-door lodging, with
access from your cabin to over 50K of trail in the closely
connected state park and Deer Yard systems. All trails are
double-tracked with a Pisten-Bully groomer.

INTERPRETIVE FEATURE
These trails start virtually from Lake Superior, climbing 600 feet
to the top of Lookout Mountain and as much as 1200 feet to the
old Cascade fire tower site in the Deer Yard trails. There are
always differences between the lakeshore and the inland hills in
terms of forest type and snow depth. What do *you* see?

RIVER TRAILS (2.2K)

EASIEST TO ADVANCED / DIAGONAL ONLY

These are classic, old-fashioned ski trails with tight turns and
abrupt, sometimes steep hills. These trails are used extensively by
hikers and snowshoers in winter (the Superior Hiking Trail shares
the trail), so use caution and a strong snowplow. Nice views of the
Cascade River gorge.

PIONEER TRAIL (6.5K)

INTERMEDIATE / DIAGONAL ONLY

This is the primary large loop of the close-in trails in the Cascade
Lodge system. The first 1.5K are on a wide roadbed, groomed for
skating and are rated easiest. After the junction with the Lookout
Mountain trail, the trail narrows and gets more difficult, with a long
herringbone climb right at the start. The trail continues with level
terrain interspersed with short climbs, past the junction with Upper

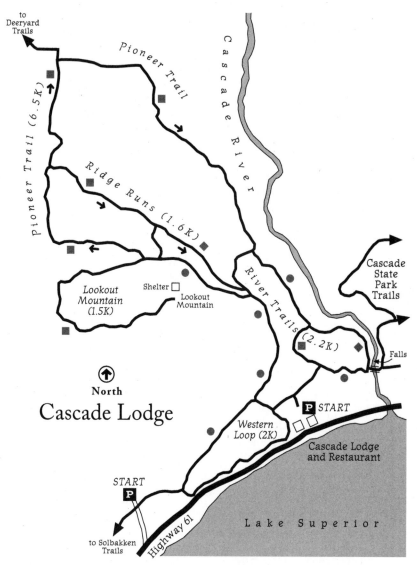

Ridge Run up to 1250 feet before descending back into the state park and to the lodge.

UPPER AND LOWER RIDGE RUNS (1.6K)
INTERMEDIATE TO ADVANCED / DIAGONAL ONLY

These are literally runs down a ridge, cutting off from the Pioneer Loop. As you approach the last leg of the Upper Ridge Run, have a good snowplow ready as you will be zooming nonstop through a

John Beargrease and race

As you work your way along these winter trails, remember John Beargrease, the Ojibway fur trapper, sailor and mail carrier who made weekly trips for twenty years from Two Harbors to Grand Marais along the old Lake Shore Trail and on the water. In early to mid January each year, watch out for modern-day mushers bearing his name (and his letters) in the 500-mile John Beargrease Sled Dog Marathon. Following the race from its start in Duluth through the rest stops and highway crossings along the way is a winter adventure in its own right, best accompanied by warm boots and big furry hats. ✳

twisting tunnel of balsam fir. There is also a challenging hill midway down the Lower Ridge Run.

LOOKOUT MOUNTAIN (1.5K)
INTERMEDIATE / DIAGONAL ONLY

Take your time on an almost 500 foot climb to the top. The trail narrows and steepens after leaving the Pioneer Trail. After the bulk of the climb, where you will have to herringbone a few times, the trail narrows and then shares space with the Superior Hiking Trail for a twisting run along the ridgetop. There is a shelter on top to rest up before the glide down. The view is nice although obscured by birch trees unless you scamper below the shelter.

WESTERN LOOP (2.0K)
EASIEST / DIAGONAL AND SKATING

This loop has multiple personalities. On the northern half you are on a wide road with double tracks groomed for skate skiing and virtually no curves. On the southern half, you are in dark woods, with significant hills and turns—and no skating. Although marked "easy," this southern half is definitely trickier than the northern, so be careful with beginners. From the western end of the loop, it's a skate-able 0.4K to a small state park parking lot, and then much further on to the Solbakken trails and the Lutsen area.

LUTSEN CONNECTOR

See Solbakken (page 100).

ASSOCIATED LODGING

Cascade Lodge provides a range of lodging opportunities including ten cabins and fourteen lodge rooms. Meals and trail lunches are available next door at the restaurant.

FOR MORE INFORMATION

Cascade Lodge, 3719 W. Highway 61, Lutsen MN 55612
(218) 387-1112 or (800) 322-9543
cascade@cascadelodgemn.com www.cascadelodgemn.com

Deer Yard

TRAILHEAD ACCESS
From Highway 61, take County Road 7 either from Grand Marais or from Milepost 100 (by Cascade River State Park, eight miles west of Grand Marais) to County Road 45, then go 4.1 miles west on 45 from intersection of County Roads 44 and 45. Turn left on Forest Road, 0.7 miles to trailhead, small parking area off a turn in the road.

TOTAL TRAIL: 17K
Groomed Diagonal: 17K   Skating: none   Lit: none

PASS REQUIREMENTS
• Great Minnesota Ski Pass

TRAILHEAD FACILITIES
None

SNOWPHONE (800) 897-7669

WHAT MAKES IT UNIQUE
This area is remote and yet very well-maintained. The variety of landscape and scenery makes for a nice all-day outing.

INTERPRETIVE FEATURE
A deer yard is an area where deer gather in large numbers during the winter, migrating up to fifty miles to find the right place. What makes this area a deer yard? Well, there is plenty of cedar, especially around Deer Yard Lake, and cedar is the deer's favorite winter food (ironically cedar is like candy to the deer: they love to eat it, but would starve from lack of essential nutrients if they ate only cedar). But some winters there are no deer here at all. Extreme snow depth can drive the deer out of this area and closer to the lake, where the snow is always a lot shallower.

DEER YARD LAKE (11.1K)

INTERMEDIATE

This is a wonderful half-day trip around a high ridge and along the cedar-lined shore of Deer Yard Lake. The truly ambitious can include this loop as part of a full-day ski up from Cascade River State Park. Traveling clockwise, you will experience a variety of forests. In the first stretch young conifers hold close to the trail. A long climb takes you into the typical North Shore maple and yellow-birch forest, then you will glide down into the old cedars of Deer Yard Lake. Stop for spring water (and check the temperature) along the way, and enjoy a break on the lake at its eastern end where a rough trail leads down onto the shore.

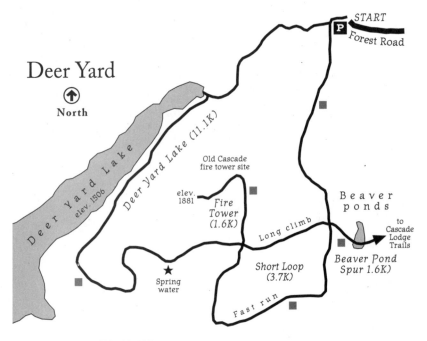

FIRE TOWER (1.6K)
ADVANCED
Climb an additional 200 feet to the former site of a fire tower from which there is a good view of Deer Yard Lake.

SHORT LOOP (3.7K)
MORE DIFFICULT TO ADVANCED
Break up your climb on the long loop or, if you are not doing the long loop, take this trail on your way back to the trailhead.

BEAVER POND SPUR (1.6K)
MORE DIFFICULT
A short run along the trail takes you to a wide-open beaver meadows, a nice contrast from the relatively dense forest of the Deer Yard Loop. This trail connects Deer Yard with the rest of the Cascade system.

FOR MORE INFORMATION
Cascade Lodge, 3719 W. Highway 61, Lutsen MN 55612
(218) 387-1112 or (800) 322-9543
cascade@cascadelodgemn.com
www.cascadelodgemn.com

Bear Track

TRAILHEAD ACCESS
From Highway 61, take Cook County Road 7 about 4 miles to
County Road 48, which joins County Road 158. Take 158 for 2.1
miles to end. Bear Track's paying guests can park at trailhead with
map; others use Superior Hiking Trail parking lot on left before
right-hand turn.

TOTAL TRAIL: 25K
Groomed Diagonal: 25K   Skating: 8K   Lit: none

PASS REQUIREMENTS
• Great Minnesota Ski Pass

TRAILHEAD FACILITIES
None. Rental and lodging registration at office on County
Road 13, 0.5 mile from Highway 61 (Rosebush Creek Ranch).

SNOWPHONE (800) 897-7669

WHAT MAKES IT UNIQUE
Rustic cabins allow overnight experiences. Although connected
to the North Shore Mountains system, this section will preserve
a traditional skiing atmosphere with narrow trails groomed by
snowmobile.

INTERPRETIVE FEATURE
This trail system demonstrates the strong symbiosis between
cross-country skiing and forest management. Many of the trails
are or were used for logging, and you pass the site of the historic
(1900) Nunstad sawmill on the Sundling Creek Loop. Most of the
western loop through the moose area is either on freshly cut
areas or in a pine plantation. Some of the best ski trails on the
North Shore were originally logging roads, and these trails are a
great example.

BRER RABBIT RUN (2.5K)
EASIER / DIAGONAL ONLY

This tight network of trails is perfect for a wandering warm-up
when you don't want to think hard but would rather focus on
skiing. The nice coniferous woods invite you to poke around.

SUNDLING CREEK LOOP (3.2K)
EASIER / DIAGONAL ONLY

This trail wanders through the woods with tight but easygoing
turns. The forest is mostly mixed birch, spruce and fir. The trail
loops around the "wildlife ponds," a large marshy area. On the

north side of the loop the trail joins an old logging road, so it widens and flattens out before the last stretch back to the trailhead.

BIDDLE BOYS TRAIL (1.0K)
ADVANCED / DIAGONAL ONLY

This trail is the exception to the generally level and easy terrain of the Bear Track trails. It rolls up and down and up and down through piney woods. It's a fun and tiring way to end a longer, easier loop.

MOOSE AREA LOOP (2.7K)
EASIER / DIAGONAL ONLY

This loop adds both distance and variety of habitat to the Sundling Creek Loop. The southern side of the loop is largely in clearings favored by moose, while the northern side of the loop (after the "Big Cedar Tree" which marks the junction with the connector trail to Cascade State Park) is largely pine plantation, with adolescent jack and red pine. This section is known locally as "Bullwinkle Run."

BALLY CREEK TRAILS (2.6K)
INTERMEDIATE / DIAGONAL ONLY

Use these trails either as a set of small loops on their own or as an intermediate connection to the Bally Creek Loop. Numerous cleared areas add to the variety and the views. The trails climb to elevations of over 1740 feet, easily some of the highest terrain in the whole North Shore skiing system, with a fantastic view to Eagle Mountain, the highest point in Minnesota.

BALLY CREEK LOOP (3.5K)
EASIER / DIAGONAL ONLY

By the time you've skied the access to this loop from the Sundling Creek Loop and skied the figure eight crisscross, you've done a total of 3.5K, not including the ungroomed 1.6K round trip to the North Shore Corridor snowmobile trail (the path of the John Beargrease Sled Dog Marathon in January).

North

Bear Track

SKATING ROAD (8K)

EASY / DIAGONAL AND SKATING

If you drove here, this is the road you came in on. As a wide and
flat Forest Service road, it's perfect for skate skiing. It's also tracked
for diagonal skiing, so bring your first-timers here and ski alongside them.

WOLF PACK RUN (CASCADE CONNECTOR) (10.4K)

INTERMEDIATE / DIAGONAL ONLY

Only the aerobically crazy will choose to ski this trail uphill, with
its 900 feet elevation gain from Cascade River State Park. Instead,
get a buddy or an innkeeper to deliver you to the Bally Creek
trailhead, ski through the Bear Track system and enjoy the nearly
1000-foot drop over 14K or more of trail. The connector takes
you through moose and wolf country with beautiful views of Lake
Superior. You can cut this in half by just doing the bottom half
from County Road 45.

ASSOCIATED LODGING

Bally Creek Camp offers wood-heated, nonsmoking rustic cabins actually within the ski trail system. Pets are welcome; a separate trail is available for skijoring. For reservations, contact the number below.

FOR MORE INFORMATION

Bear Track Outfitting Co.
Box 937, Grand Marais MN 55604
(218) 387-1162 or (800) 795-8068
outfitters@bear-track.com
www.bear-track.com

Critters under the snow

What's the most common animal in these woods? It's the tiny shrew. Tucked underneath that white cloak of snow is a busy network of trails dug by little critters like the shrew and the voles. These tunnels help tiny critters to survive in two ways: the tunnels protect the shrews and voles from the sight of predators and they keep them warm, using the insulating power of snow to keep a "room temperature" close to freezing even when the temperature "outside" is much colder.

❄

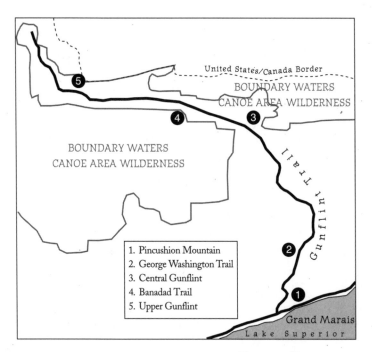

United States/Canada Border

BOUNDARY WATERS
CANOE AREA WILDERNESS

BOUNDARY WATERS
CANOE AREA WILDERNESS

Gunflint Trail

1. Pincushion Mountain
2. George Washington Trail
3. Central Gunflint
4. Banadad Trail
5. Upper Gunflint

Grand Marais
Lake Superior

Gunflint Trail Cross-Country Ski Trails

Take a short drive up and away from the North Shore to skiers' heaven. This is the Boundary Waters, with remote lakes and "Canadian" weather. The resorts of the Gunflint Trail have assembled a pure skiing experience, from their dueling Pisten-Bully groomers to the saunas and wax rooms. Whether you are circling the lakes in the Central Gunflint, climbing the ridges of the Upper Gunflint, or curving around Pincushion Mountain, you will be immersed in skiing and skiing only. Take a trip down the Banadad Trail, staying in a yurt halfway along, and you will complete the Gunflint experience.

Pincushion Mountain

TRAILHEAD ACCESS
Take Gunflint Trail 1.7 miles north of Grand Marais from Highway 61 and enter the Pincushion trailhead on right. Registered B&B guests can enter from Pincushion Bed & Breakfast a little farther up.

TOTAL TRAIL: 23K
Groomed Diagonal: 23K   Skating: 23K   Lit: none

PASS REQUIREMENTS
- Great Minnesota Ski Pass
- Recommended membership in North Superior Ski and Run Club ($10/individual, $20/family, address page 118).

TRAILHEAD FACILITIES
Outhouse at public trailhead.

SNOWPHONE (800) 897-7669 OR (888) 922-2221

WHAT MAKES IT UNIQUE
These trails have a real community feel to them, from the nonskiers sharing the trailhead view to the sign describing the support of Grand Marais businesses. These are some of the only trails on the shore designed by skiers specifically for skiers, and it shows.

INTERPRETIVE FEATURE
Unless you stay in the very inner loops, you can't help but notice the birch trees here. Look at their bark against a snowy hillside, and you may notice that the bark is not a pure white but has a reddish tinge. The birch is a tree that indicates change. Many of the birch stands on the North Shore grew up following severe fires in the 1920s. Now these stands are dying, due to old age and diseases. The Pincushion birches seem to be in good health…so enjoy!

OVERLOOK LOOPS (2.3K)

EASIER

These two loops start and end at the public trailhead and are named for their location near this overlook rather than any view from the trails themselves. The West Overlook Loop, at 1.3K is part of the main trail connecting the trailhead with the inner trails; a steady climb starts it off. The East Overlook Loop, at 1K, is separated from the rest of the traffic but is a little hillier than the west loop, making it less suited for real beginners.

PINCUSHION MOUNTAIN LOOP (6.8K)
INTERMEDIATE

Follow the clear signage through the first four intersections as you head out on this loop. Although rated intermediate, this trail is relatively easy skiing and provides a nice morning or afternoon outing through a mature birch forest. Much of the section over the river is also the Superior Hiking Trail. Stretch out the day by snacking at the shelter overlooking the Devil Track River valley and taking off your skis to walk 1/4 mile to the top of Pincushion Mountain itself for a wide view of Lake Superior.

NORTH ADVANCED LOOP (4.1K)
ADVANCED

This loop is carved out of the hilly central section of the trail system; once again, the clear signs allow you to skip reading maps and just follow the arrows. Ski this loop a couple of times and watch for the transition into and out of a nearly pure birch forest from a mixture of aspen, spruce and fir.

B&B LOOP (1K)
EASIER

This trail is perfect for guests of Pincushion B&B to try out their skills before heading out on the advanced trails. The B&B Loop is lit by kerosene lanterns for Pincushion guests on Saturday nights.

CANYON CURVES LOOP (1.8K)
INTERMEDIATE

This trail lives up to its name right away as you descend from the B&B Loop down a curvy trail. The trail loops and turns through birch and fir before a final run along the rim of the Little Devil Track River. Take a second loop around before you grunt back up the hill.

OLE HYVAA AND HILFIKER HILL LOOPS (2.9K)
ADVANCED

These are rolling trails in the tradition of adventurous Nordic skiing, as seen in their names. The 1.9K Ole Hyvaa Loop is loosely translated from the Finnish for "Oh my God!" The 1K Hilfiker Hill Loop is named after Dr. Hilfiker, an early ski enthusiast who lived near the trails in the early 1970s. Parts of these loops may be shared with the Superior Hiking Trail.

SCHOOL CONNECTOR (2.8K)
ADVANCED

Although not always groomed, this trail provides an easy opportunity for "norpine" skiing, connecting the public trailhead with the Grand Marais school complex below. It is also the last stretch of the Sawtooth ski race each January.

ASSOCIATED LODGING
Pincushion Bed & Breakfast was built and is managed by skiers for skiers. Four cozy guest rooms are available.

FOR MORE INFORMATION
Pincushion Mountain Bed & Breakfast
968 Gunflint Trail
Grand Marais MN 55604
(218) 387-1276

North Superior Ski and Run Club
PO Box 542
Grand Marais MN 55604

Art galleries in Grand Marais

A great way to round out your winter experience is with a visit to one of Grand Marais' art galleries. Check out the local and Inuit art at Sivertson's Gallery on Wisconsin Street. The Sivertson family has been an institution on the North Shore and Isle Royale since the turn of the century, first as fishermen and now as artists. ❄

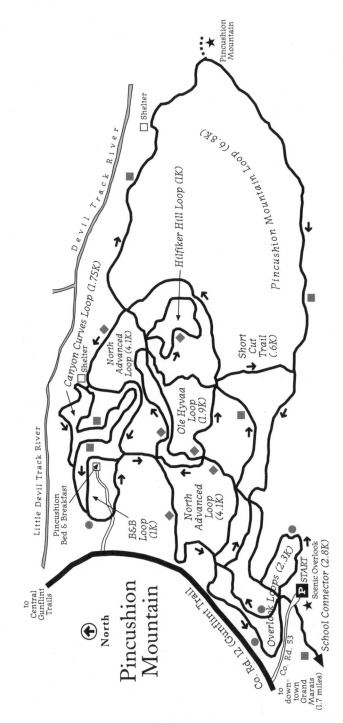

Pincushion Mountain

Devil Track River

Little Devil Track River

Shelter

Canyon Curves Loop (1.75K)

Shelter

North Advanced Loop (4.1K)

Hilfiker Hill Loop (1K)

Pincushion Mountain Loop (6.8K)

Short Cut Trail (.6K)

Ole Hyvaa Loop (1.9K)

to Central Gunflint Trails

North Advanced Loop (4.1K)

Pincushion Bed & Breakfast

B&B Loop (1K)

Pincushion Mountain

North

Co. Rd. 12 (Gunflint Trail)

Co. Rd. 53

Overlook Loops (2.3K)

P START

Scenic Overlook

School Connector (2.8K)

to downtown Grand Marais (1.7 miles)

George Washington Trail

TRAILHEAD ACCESS
Take Gunflint Trail 6.4 miles from Highway 61 to parking lot on left.

TOTAL TRAIL: 3.5K
Groomed Diagonal: 3.5K   Skating: none   Lit: none

PASS REQUIREMENTS
• None

TRAILHEAD FACILITIES
None

WHAT MAKES IT UNIQUE
This gentle, infrequently groomed little loop provides a quiet alternative to the large trail systems typical to the Gunflint region.

INTERPRETIVE FEATURE
This pine plantation was planted in 1932 by Boy Scouts from Grand Marais to reforest an area hard hit by logging and fires.

North

George Washington Trail

to Central and Upper Gunflint Trails

START
P

Main Loop (3.5K)

Elbow Creek

Old road

Gunflint Trail

to Grand Marais and Pincushion Mountain Trails

MAIN LOOP (3.5K)

EASIER

Although groomed only occasionally, this simple loop is used often enough by both local skiers and respectful snowshoers that you can generally count on there being a decent trail. The counterclockwise loop starts and ends in the pine plantation for which it is named, but along the way there is a wide variety of forest types, as well as mellow little Elbow Creek.

FOR MORE INFORMATION
USFS Gunflint Ranger Station, PO Box 790 Grand Marais MN 55604 (218) 387-1750

Central Gunflint

TRAILHEAD ACCESS

There are two trailheads. Take the Gunflint Trail to:
(1) Golden Eagle Lodge—28 miles from Grand Marais, right on Clearwater Road for 3.5 miles; or (2) Bearskin Lodge—26 miles from Grand Marais, right at sign.

TOTAL TRAIL: 63K

Groomed Diagonal: 63K   Skating: 28K   Lit: 2.1K

PASS REQUIREMENTS

Jointly managed by Bearskin and Golden Eagle Lodges.
• Free for guests of lodges. For others, day passes ($10/day or $7.50/half day) and season passes ($60/adult, $30/child) available at trailheads. Ticket sharing and shuttle with Upper Gunflint available.

TRAILHEAD FACILITIES

Full facilities at both trailheads, including snacks and ski rental.

SNOWPHONE (800) 897-7669

WHAT MAKES IT UNIQUE

As with the Upper Gunflint system, multiple private facilities have cooperated to develop an excellent and vast network of trails ideally suited for a cross-country ski vacation.

INTERPRETIVE FEATURE

The geology here is quite different from that found on the North Shore itself. The Rove Formation is a sedimentary deposit, at 1.8 billion years old much older than the dark diabase, known as the Logan intrusions, which squeezed into it during the same time the volcanic rocks of the North Shore were forming. The result is alternating bands of hard diabase and soft shales and graywacke; the softer rock has eroded and formed into basins, which filled with water and are the lakes you will ski around or over. The Logan intrusions are the scenic hills you climb.

OLD LOGGING CAMP (10.7K)

EASIEST TO ADVANCED / DIAGONAL AND SKATING

This is the main part of a 13–14K loop around Flour Lake. East of Golden Eagle Lodge the trail follows an old logging railroad (except for one detour onto Flour Lake) leading to the site of a historic logging camp, complete with "timber jays." The 3.7K below the North Flour loops is groomed for skate skiing. After a brief passage over the boundary of the BWCA, the trail disappears into the Bearskin-area trail network. The trail reemerges on the west end of Rudy Lake for a wild ride on top of glacial eskers around the end of Flour Lake.

WOLF POINT (0.6K)
INTERMEDIATE / DIAGONAL ONLY / LIT

This is Golden Eagle Lodge's night skiing loop, lit by kerosene lanterns on some nights and electric lights on others. The hills that are fun by day are thrilling at night.

NORTH FLOUR LOOPS (6.7K)
ADVANCED / DIAGONAL AND SKATING

Three side trails roll off an easy section of the Old Logging Camp Trail. Each trail climbs 120–150 feet to ridges with views both south over the lakes and north into Canada. The Red Pine loops total 3K, lead through a young red pine forest and have a shelter on top with a view of West Bearskin Lake. The Cross Fox Trail has 1.7K of varied terrain and some old-growth white pine. Finally, Moose Ridge offers Canadian views and a roller coaster ride back down to Old Logging Camp Trail.

MOOSE PASTURE (1.1K)
EASIER / DIAGONAL AND SKATING

These open woods are the result of forest management and provide good winter habitat for moose. You may be accosted by gray jays here; bring some extra snacks just in case.

OVERLOOK TRAIL (1.2K)
EASIER / DIAGONAL AND SKATING

Extend your hunt for moose uphill to this open area, and take the short trail to the overlook on Flour Lake.

RIDGE RUN TRAIL (6K)
INTERMEDIATE TO ADVANCED / DIAGONAL ONLY

This new trail runs along the ridge overlooking Flour Lake. Watch for sharp turns and great views. The overlook on Flour Lake is dramatic and could make you say, "It looks just like the Boundary Waters!"

BEAVER DAM TRAIL (9K)
EASIER TO INTERMEDIATE / DIAGONAL ONLY

Loop clockwise around Rudy and Ruby Lakes on this varied trail.

There are some wild downhills along the southern part of the loop. Watch for spruce swamps, beaver meadows and other boreal wetlands. There is a shelter halfway around, overlooking Flour Lake.

NORTH-SOUTH LINK (2.4K)
ADVANCED / DIAGONAL AND SKATING

Although half of this trail is on the flat surface of lakes, it earns an advanced rating partially because of some steep hills and partially because of the potential hazards of lake skiing. Stay on the groomed trails and, if in doubt (e.g. in December or April), ask at one of the lodges before heading out.

SUMMER HOME ROAD / CAMPGROUND (5K)
EASIER / DIAGONAL AND SKATING / PARTIALLY LIT

This is a central corridor for the trails centered on Bearskin Lodge, and because it is built on roads, it can be groomed more aggressively than other sections. When conditions are marginal everywhere else in northern Minnesota, this may be the only decent skiing you will find. It is wide and level, good for families and beginners. The Campground Trails are great for just goofing around. Note: A combination of the starts for Beaver Dam Trail, Summer Home Road and North-South Link form a 1.5K loop lit at night by a string of Christmas lights.

OX CART TRAIL (4K)
EASIER TO INTERMEDIATE / DIAGONAL ONLY

This "lollipop loop" is mostly easy, intimate skiing. Since it's groomed only for diagonal stride, classical skiers can enjoy the quiet woods at their own pace. After crossing a beaver pond, the trail climbs gently into pine woods. Watch for two "two-headed" trees, one pine and one spruce. Take the whole loop back to the lodge and you've skied 5.2K.

BEAR CUB WORLD CUP (8K)
ADVANCED / DIAGONAL AND SKATING

If you want a wild ride and are ready to push for it, this is the trail to test your abilities. Think Lycra and wild aerodynamic sunglasses. The trail is one of the only in this system designed specifically for challenging skate skiing, including steep uphills and "screaming" downhills.

POPLAR CREEK (8.4K)
EASIER TO INTERMEDIATE / DIAGONAL ONLY
This loop makes for a round trip of 10.2K from the junction with the Oxcart Trail. The loop takes you away from the main network of trails, across the Gunflint Trail into a quiet country of small lakes, bogs and meandering streams. A shelter halfway around makes a nice break on a day-long outing. The northern part of this section is also the beginning of the Banadad Trail (see page 126).

LACE LAKE (5K)
See Banadad Trail (page 129).

ASSOCIATED LODGING
Golden Eagle Lodge and Bearskin Lodge both offer excellent accommodations for skiers and direct access to the trails they jointly manage.

FOR MORE INFORMATION
Golden Eagle Lodge
Gunflint Trail
468 Clearwater Road
Grand Marais MN 55604
(218) 388-2203 or (800) 346-2203
ski@golden-eagle.com
www.golden-eagle.com

Bearskin Lodge
Gunflint Trail
124 E. Bearskin Road
Grand Marais MN 55604
(218) 388-2292 or (800) 338-4170

Raven-wolf interaction
These two symbols of the North Woods have a surprisingly complex relationship. If you come across a wolf-killed deer more than a few hours old, chances are you will find raven tracks along with the wolf tracks. Look for the distinctive imprint of their wing feathers in the snow as they take off in flight. It's obvious that ravens feed on wolf kills; they have been known to follow wolf tracks in the snow from the air until they find a kill site. But there is also some evidence that ravens will lead wolves to their prey; the raven use their aerial surveillance to spot animals and somehow lead the wolves to the deer. If you see a large flock of ravens near the ground, chances are there is a wolf kill, and maybe a wolf, nearby.

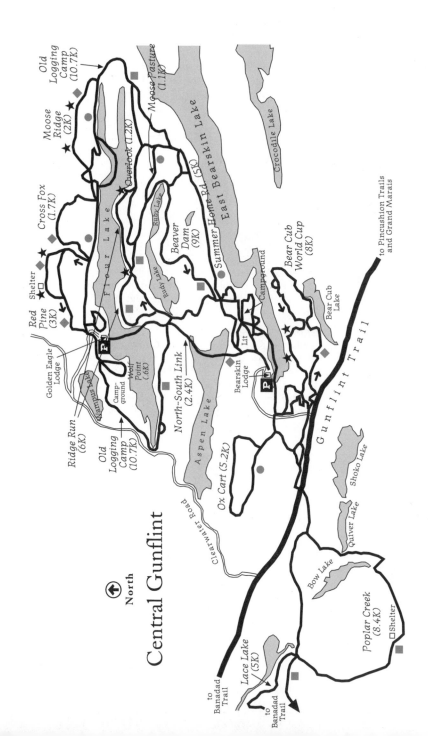

Central Gunflint

North

to Banadad Trail

Golden Eagle Lodge

Red Pine (3K)

Shelter

Cross Fox (1.7K)

Moose Ridge (2K)

Old Logging Camp (10.7K)

Overlook (1.2K)

Moose Pasture (1.1K)

Crocodile Lake

Fleur Lake

Ruby Lake

Beaver Dam (9K)

East Bearskin Lake

Summer Home Rd. (5K)

Ridge Run (6K)

Old Logging Camp (10.7K)

Krampus Lake

Campground

Wolf Point (.6K)

North-South Link (2.4K)

Aspen Lake

Campground

Lit

Bearskin Lodge

Bear Cub World Cup (8K)

Bear Cub Lake

Gunflint Trail

to Pincushion Trails and Grand Marais

Ox Cart (5.2K)

Clearwater Road

Shoko Lake

Quiver Lake

Bow Lake

Poplar Creek (8.4K)

Shelter

Lace Lake (5K)

to Banadad Trail

to Banadad Trail

Banadad Trail

TRAILHEAD ACCESS
There are four trailheads (starting closest to Grand Marais):
(1) Bearskin Lodge, with parking fee; (2) Trail Center, with parking fee; (3) Rib Lake Road, 0.25 mile southeast of Loon Lake Public Landing; (4) Upper Gunflint lodges.

TOTAL TRAIL: 43K
Groomed Diagonal: 43K   Skating: none   Lit: none

PASS REQUIREMENTS
• Great Minnesota Ski Pass
• BWCA Wilderness day-use permit (available at wilderness boundary or through outfitters).

TRAILHEAD FACILITIES
See descriptions for Upper and Central Gunflint.

SNOWPHONE (800) 897-7669

WHAT MAKES IT UNIQUE
This is the region's premiere wilderness trail experience, providing a wonderful combination of groomed trails and deep wilderness.

INTERPRETIVE FEATURE
The further you get from roads and other human impact, the more likely you are to see signs of certain reclusive northwoods animals such as the wolf and lynx, and birds such as the great gray and boreal owl. Keep an eye out for tracks during the day. If you are staying at the yurts and out for an evening ski, watch for the critters themselves, as they are often more active at dusk.

BANADAD TRAIL (27K)

Here it is, the ultimate combination of groomed trail and wilderness skiing. The Banadad Trail is 27K of nearly pure wilderness experience. Most skiers will want to or need to break up the trip by staying overnight either in a yurt or a cabin operated by Boundary Country Trekking. "Banadad" means "lost" in Anishinabe, but don't worry: the trail is well marked and well groomed.

The trail is all on land, not on lakes, so slush is not a factor. For a few miles in the middle, the trail follows the Laurentian Divide, which separates the Lake Superior watershed from the Hudson Bay watershed. In the western end, look for beaver ponds, while throughout the trail you will find open spruce bogs and dense forest. Cliffs parallel the trail at times.

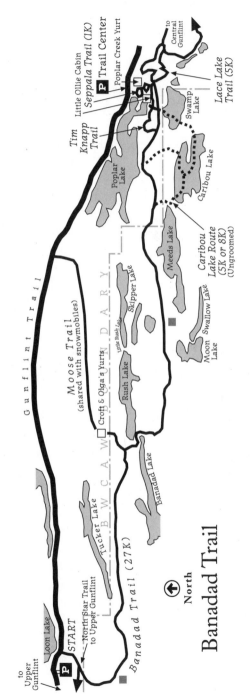

Banadad Trail

Seeing a wolf kill

As you zoom along a ski trail, an odd feeling shakes you particularly alert to your surroundings. At first you notice a tuft of brown or white hair loose in the breeze…and maybe an odd combination of critter tracks, like deer and raven. Perhaps there is a grove of cedar trees ahead. You feel a tingle in your spine. Then, not just a tuft of brown hair is visible but a clump of skin, too. The groomed ski track fades under a chaos of trails: comb-marks from the wingtips of loaded ravens taking off and wolf scat, fresh enough that it is still brown and moist. In the cedars, you see what's left of a white-tailed deer. You hear the ravens in the trees, squawking. You wonder where the wolves crouch, watching as you gingerly ski around their prey. The scene marks the end of one life as well as the continuance of many others. ❋

The trail was created in the early 1980s out of logging roads left over from before 1978, the year logging was banned in the BWCA. The old roadbed provides a smooth skiing surface, and remnants of old logging camps give you history to ponder. Before the major national long-distance ski races became dominated by skaters, the Banadad was often used as training for races such as the Birkebeiner. But no one should race through this wonderful country anymore. Take your time and enjoy a backcountry classic.

You can arrange a shuttle with the lodges or take the scheduled shuttle van.

MOOSE TRAIL (APPX. 10K)
EASIER
This is primarily an access trail for gear and equipment going to Croft and Olga's Yurts. It is sometimes groomed for diagonal skiing and can be used for skate skiing most of the time. You will encounter snowmobiles on this trail.

CARIBOU LAKE ROUTE (5K OR 8K)
ADVANCED
If you are one of those for whom the Banadad is not wild enough, add on the Caribou Lake "route" to your itinerary. This is an ungroomed route utilizing frozen lakes and the canoe portages between them.

SEPPALA AND TIM KNOPP TRAILS (2.8K)
EASIER

These trails are well suited for those guests staying at the Poplar Creek Yurt or Little Ollie Cabin who want to stretch their legs for a morning ski. The Seppala Trail also provides a connection to the Gunflint Trail and the Trail Center restaurant (the former Poplar Lake Lodge). The Tim Knopp Trail, named for a University of Minnesota professor and skier vital to the recent renaissance of skiing, is the only part of the Banadad system groomed for skate skiing. This grooming stops before the BWCA boundary.

LACE LAKE (5K)
EASIER TO INTERMEDIATE

The casual visitor to Banadad country may ski this loop as part of a day's outing from Bearskin Lodge. This loop takes you right up to the edge of the BWCA and along scenic Poplar Creek.

ASSOCIATED LODGING
Boundary Country Trekking offers both a ski-in cabin and ski-in yurts along the trail. Contact them at the numbers below. Old Northwood Lodge offers lodging and access to the Banadad Trail.

FOR MORE INFORMATION
Boundary Country Trekking
7925 Gunflint Trail
Grand Marais MN 55604
(218) 388-9972 or (800) 322-8327
bct@boreal.org
www.boreal.org/adventures/

Old Northwood Lodge
7969 Northwoods Loop
Grand Marais MN 55604
(218) 388-9464 or (800) 682-8264

Upper Gunflint

TRAILHEAD ACCESS
Take the Gunflint Trail to the Upper Gunflint lodges (see below). Once you have a pass, you can start at Loon Lake Boat Access or the Scenic Overlook on the Gunflint Trail, in addition to the lodges.

TOTAL TRAIL: 70.5K
Groomed Diagonal: 66K   Skating: 23.9K   Lit: 4K

PASS REQUIREMENTS
• Passes available at all resorts ($5/day, $10/three days or $25/ week). Price includes trail map. Pass system is shared with Central Gunflint and provides shuttle between areas.

TRAILHEAD FACILITIES
Full facilities at resort trailheads. Rental available at Gunflint Lodge. All skiers should check in and buy their passes at the resorts.

SNOWPHONE (800) 897-7669

WHAT MAKES IT UNIQUE
Along with the Central Gunflint system, the Upper Gunflint system is an amazing skiing resource, with ski-from-your-door convenience and an incredible variety of terrain.

INTERPRETIVE FEATURE
The resorts here claim to have "Canadian weather," which makes sense given that Canada is on the other side of Gunflint Lake. In a typical year, over 100 inches of snow fall, the highest average snowfall in the state. In addition, the lakes stay frozen longer than anywhere else in the state which, with the snow, helps secure late-season skiing. The cold is much more pronounced than by the shore of Lake Superior, so come prepared!

Northwest trails

MAGNETIC ROCK (4K ONE-WAY)
INTERMEDIATE TO ADVANCED / DIAGONAL ONLY
From the intersciion with the Cut Across Trail, this remote trail leads past a small pond, a fire burn and a 60-foot high glacial erratic that will make your compass needle swing. Open vistas at the west end of the trail make nice rest areas before turning back.

WARRENS ROAD (4.2K) / CUT ACROSS TRAIL (1.6K) / LANTERN TRAIL (2K)
EASIER TO INTERMEDIATE / DIAGONAL ONLY / LIT
Warrens Road is an easy and fast double tracked trail from a gravel

pit to a three-way intersection with the Magnetic Rock Trail. The Cut Across Trail is rated more difficult, but the cautious beginner should have no problem (and should have some fun) on these gradual hills. A 2K lantern-lit trail (not shown on map) loops off the Cut-Across Trail back to Borderland Lodge.

ASPEN ALLEY / RIVER TRAIL (3.2K)
EASIER TO INTERMEDIATE / DIAGONAL ONLY

These two trails combine on either side of the Gunflint Trail for a relatively easy, open country loop. The River Trail, on the north side, is better suited for more experienced skiers.

POWER LINE (2.4K)
EASIEST / DIAGONAL ONLY

This double tracked trail escorts beginners from Borderland Lodge and makes for an accessible loop through Aspen Alley, Warrens Road and the Cut Across Trail.

Corridor Trail

WEST END TRAIL (6.5K)
INTERMEDIATE TO ADVANCED / DIAGONAL AND SKATING

This is a double tracked main corridor trail connecting Border-land Lodge on the north with Loon Lake and the Gunflint Trail on the south. Along the way the trail is hilly and challenging.

Northeast trails

BIG PINE (3.2K)
EASIER TO INTERMEDIATE / DIAGONAL ONLY

Dramatic scenery and lots of wildlife sign make this double tracked loop a great introduction to skiing Gunflint-style.

LITTLE PINE (2K)
EASIER TO INTERMEDIATE / DIAGONAL ONLY / LIT

This is a small loop trail between Gunflint Lodge and Gunflint Pines (not shown on map) and is lit each night. It is a great warm-up trail in the morning or an evening final fling to watch the northern lights.

OVERLOOK (0.8K)
EASIER TO INTERMEDIATE / DIAGONAL AND SKATING
This short, hilly, double tracked trail is your access to not only the scenic overlook but all the trails on the south side of the Gunflint Trail. You'll climb 120 feet from the junction with the Big Pine Trail to the overlook…and it's worth it.

RABBIT RUN (5.6K)
EASIER TO INTERMEDIATE / DIAGONAL AND SKATING
Branching off the West End Trail, this double tracked trail runs along the bottom of a glacial ridge, crosses the Gunflint, then parallels the Highlands Trail below the 140-foot cliff. The dense forest provides protective habitat for moose and deer. A warming hut is located near the intersection with the West End Trail.

SOUTH RIM (4.8K)
INTERMEDIATE TO ADVANCED / DIAGONAL ONLY
Scoot along the top of a ridge with dramatic views of Gunflint Lake 400 feet below and the Canadian hills beyond. You could use the Lonely Lake Trail as part of a round trip back. Steep hills at both ends keep this section in the advanced category.

LONELY LAKE (4.8K)
EASIER TO INTERMEDIATE / DIAGONAL ONLY
This double tracked trail runs parallel to the South Rim Trail, no more than 150 yards away but 200 feet below. There are old-growth white pines and nice views of Gunflint and Lonely Lakes. A warming hut is located near the west end of the trail.

AMPERAGE WAY (4.5K)
INTERMEDIATE / SKATING AND SKIJORING ONLY
This trail parallels Lonely Lake Trail. Groomed eight-feet wide with no diagonal track, it's meant for skaters and skijorers. The trail goes through a deep, thick cedar swamp.

Trails south of the Gunflint Trail

HIGHLANDS TRAIL (6.5K)
INTERMEDIATE TO ADVANCED / DIAGONAL AND SKATING
Hills at both ends of this double tracked trail bracket a high-country run with nice views all along. The preferred travel direction is from

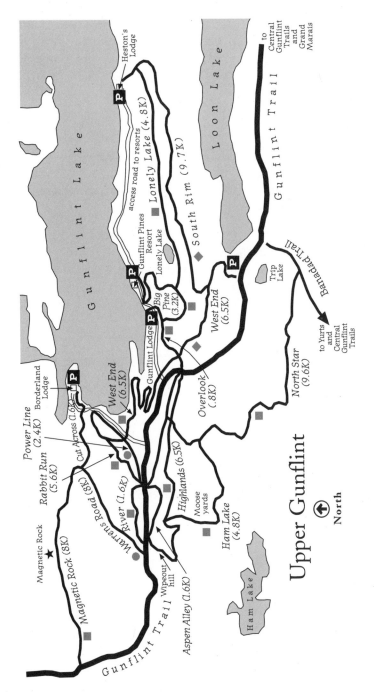

Upper Gunflint

Heston's Lodge

Loon Lake

to Central Gunflint Trails and Grand Marais

Gunflint Trail

Lonely Lake (4.8K)

access road to resorts

South Rim (9.7K)

Gunflint Pines Resort

Lonely Lake

Gunflint Lake

Big Pine (3.2K)

West End (6.5K)

Trip Lake

Barracade Trail

to Yurts and Central Gunflint Trails

Gunflint Lodge

West End (6.5K)

Borderland Lodge

Overlook (.8K)

North Star (9.6K)

Power Line (2.4K)

Rabbit Run (5.6K)

Cut Across (1.6K)

Warrens Road (8K)

River (1.6K)

Highlands (6.5K)

Moose yards

Magnetic Rock

Magnetic Rock (8K)

Wipeout hill

Aspen Alley (1.6K)

Ham Lake (4.8K)

Ham Lake

Gunflint Trail

North

east to west, allowing you to pause for nice views as you climb from the scenic overlook on the Gunflint Trail and providing for the full experience of Wipeout Hill, an "S" curve with a drop of over 120 feet to the Cross River below.

HAM LAKE TRAIL (4.8K)
EASIER TO INTERMEDIATE / DIAGONAL ONLY
Take a detour from the Highlands Trail and get into some serious moose country. The gently rolling, double tracked terrain is well suited for novice skiers, and when a cold wind is blowing through the open country, the warming hut will come in handy for a snack break.

NORTH STAR (9.6K)
INTERMEDIATE / DIAGONAL ONLY
Diverse habitats mark this single tracked feeder trail to the Banadad Trail, with forestry management areas, wetlands and dense forests. As with the other trails on this side of the Gunflint, there is a good chance to see wildlife here.

ASSOCIATED LODGING
The lodges listed below all provide excellent accommodations for skiers.

FOR MORE INFORMATION
Borderland Lodge
194 N. Gunflint Lake Road, Grand Marais MN 55604
(218) 388-2233 or (800) 451-1667

Gunflint Lodge
143 S. Gunflint Lake Road, Grand Marais MN 55604
(218) 388-2294 or (800) 328-3325
gunflint@gunflint.com, www.gunflint.com

Gunflint Pines Resort
217 S. Gunflint Lake Road, Grand Marais MN 55604
(218) 388-4454 or (800) 533-5814

Heston's Lodge
840 Gunflint Trail, Grand Marais MN 55604
(218) 388-2243 or (800) 338-7230

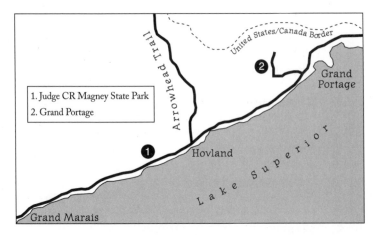

1. Judge CR Magney State Park
2. Grand Portage

United States/Canada Border

Arrowhead Trail

Grand Portage

Hovland

Lake Superior

Grand Marais

The Far Shore Cross-Country Ski Trails

Two remote ski areas and one urban area combine to end the North Shore ski experience. Grand Portage is rich in tradition, with an ideal combination of groomed and wilderness skiing in an area long known for its trails. Judge C.R. Magney State Park provides an intimate outing far from the crowds. In the Thunder Bay area, six very different options await, making a special ski trip to this bustling city quite worthwhile.

Judge C.R. Magney State Park

TRAILHEAD ACCESS
The park is 14 miles east of Grand Marais on Highway 61.
Take the main park road past the guard station to the end.

TOTAL TRAIL: 5.5K
Groomed Diagonal: 5.5K   Skating: none   Lit: none

PASS REQUIREMENTS
• Great Minnesota Ski Pass
• Minnesota State Parks vehicle permit

TRAILHEAD FACILITIES
Outhouse

WHAT MAKES IT UNIQUE
This combination of intimate trails with frequent grooming is
unique to this end of the North Shore.

INTERPRETIVE FEATURE
The Brule River, which flows through this park, comes from
Brule Lake in the BWCA. Believe it or not, the Temperance River
also comes from Brule Lake, but enters Lake Superior more than
forty miles southwest of here.

LONG LOOP (4.1K)

INTERMEDIATE

This is a double "lollipop" loop, with an access "stick" of 1.3K
(which is also the Superior Hiking Trail) followed by a 2.2K loop,
on which is added a 0.6K "stick" to a small loop at the shelter. You
will climb a total of 340 feet. On the way in you will pass a nice
stand of white pine. The first loop lets you ski along the bank of
Gauthier Creek and an open spruce meadow, while the second
provides the only view of this loop, with two overlooks on the
Brule River, including one from the shelter at the end of the loop.
Depending on annual funding, the west part of the loop may or
may not be groomed.

SHORT LOOP (1.4K)

INTERMEDIATE

Although this loop is short, it packs a punch, with a 120-foot
climb to the top and a scenic downhill run overlooking the Brule
River and Lake Superior. A bench is available in low snow condi-

tions to take a break. The small shrubs and trees within the mostly birch forest are mountain maple, which indicates this is a boreal forest.

FOR MORE INFORMATION
Judge C.R. Magney State Park
Grand Marais MN 55604
(218) 387-2929

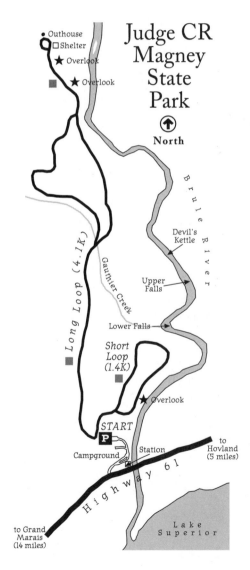

Grand Portage

TRAILHEAD ACCESS
Take County Road 17 and County Road 89 five miles north and west of Highway 61 to trail center and parking lot on left.

TOTAL TRAIL: 24K
Groomed Diagonal: 24K   Skating: 24K   Lit: none

PASS REQUIREMENTS
• Great Minnesota Ski Pass required

TRAILHEAD FACILITIES
Ski rental and outhouse.

WHAT MAKES IT UNIQUE
In addition to the 24K of groomed trails described below, a wide selection of long, ungroomed loops to scenic locations makes this a wilderness skier's heaven.

INTERPRETIVE FEATURE
The extensive maple stands here are one of the farthest north known. The hills in the area, such as Mount Sophie, are made of erosion-resistant gabbro and diabase, which also forms Hat Point and Pigeon Point on Lake Superior below.

INNER LOOPS (NIKA, WARM-UP) (3K)

INTERMEDIATE

These two loops are right at the trailhead and provide a quick warm-up loop to test your wax before heading out. They are not for beginners, however, especially Nika with a serious downhill on the return side. Nika, by the way, is Anishinabe for "wild goose."

SAWMILL (4K)

EASIER

Climb gradually from the trailhead along the main corridor trail, then return through open fields. You will peel off of this loop for most of the other options in this system.

MOUNT SOPHIE (8K)

INTERMEDIATE

This loop when taken from the trailhead totals 11.3K and travels two distinct types of forest, with maple all the way in to Mount Sophie and boreal forest with wetlands all the way out. You will want to take the 0.7K spur up to the top of Mount Sophie, though

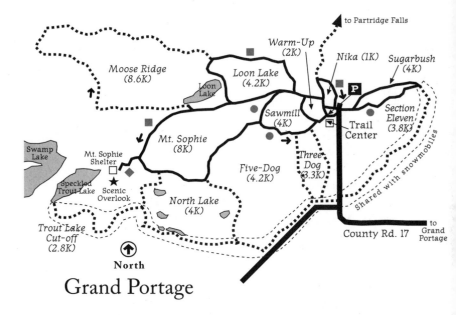

Grand Portage

you have to herringbone most of the way up. The view is breath-taking. There is a cabin there that has been closed to overnight use but still provides a nice place to rest. For the truly brave, a wind-swept fire tower awaits on top as well. The scariest part of the main loop, a winding downhill run, comes right after the Mount Sophie spur.

LOON LAKE (4.2K)

INTERMEDIATE

From where this loop leaves the Mount Sophie Trail, it's 4.2K back to the Nika Trail and the trail center, through a maple forest that has been tapped by the Anishinabe for centuries. You could encounter some tired and snowy skiers in the middle of the loop as they come off the ungroomed Moose Ridge Loop. There are sce-nic overlooks of Loon Lake and of the Partridge Creek valley. At the end, watch for a long fast downhill with a 90-degree turn in it.

SUGARBUSH (4K)

EASIER

This is an easy loop perfect for the beginner through a substantial stand of maple.

UNGROOMED TRAILS

In addition to these groomed trails, there are another 22K of ungroomed trails that lead off to remote corners. The Three Dog and Moose Ridge loops are for skiers only, while the southern sections of North Lake and Five-Dog trails are shared with snow-mobiles. The Trout Lake Cut-Off and Section Eleven trails are shared with snowmobiles. Also, some people ski the historic Grand Portage itself. Inquire locally before heading off on these trails.

ASSOCIATED LODGING

Grand Portage Lodge is not just for casino gamblers. Contact them at the address below.

FOR MORE INFORMATION

Grand Portage Lodge
Box 307
Grand Portage MN 55605
(218) 475-2401 or (800) 232-1384

Skiing across the border

It would not be fair to North Shore skiers to leave out the excellent trails around Thunder Bay. Like the Duluth-Superior area, this metropolitan area has ski areas ranging from the small and rustic to the large and elaborate. Head across the border for a day or a week, enjoy the ethnic flavor of Thunder Bay and some fun, varied skiing.

Come in January for the Northern Lights Winter Carnival. Stoke up for your day's outing with a breakfast of Finnish pancakes at the Hoito on Bay Street. If it's just too cold, visit the Thunder Bay Historical Museum, and its stellar collection of Ojibwa crafts, on Donald Street. Or just take in the view of the Sleeping Giant.

WHERE TO SKI

On the north side of Thunder Bay, off the 11/17 expressway, you will find **Centennial Park,** with 15K of remote-feeling, mostly diagonal skiing, and loops ranging from 4K to 10K. The trails are on the easier side. Fee box at trailhead. Park phone (807) 625-2351.

Out at **Kakabeka Falls Provincial Park**, north and west of town, there are 15K of easier to intermediate trails. Four loops ranging from 1.5K to 9K in length provide a variety of terrain and wonderful views. Though the trails are relatively narrow, both skate skiing and diagonal skiing are possible. Fee box at trailhead. Park phone (807) 475-7081.

Kamview Nordic Centre provides 24K of easier to intermediate trails, including 5K that is lit. Eight different loops take you to dramatic views of the Nor'Wester Mountains, Lake Superior and the Kaministiquia River valley. To reach Kamview, turn north on the 20th Sideroad off Highway 61 south of town. Fee box at trailhead. Phone (807) 475-7081.

Carved out of the urban wilderness of Thunder Bay, the 5K of trails at **Lakehead University** cut through the campus and the adjacent country club golf course. There's a surprising variety of terrain. Go to the university fieldhouse, at the corner of Oliver and Golf Links Road, for tickets and the trailhead. Phone (807) 343-8585.

Olympic skier Reijo Puiras designed and owns **Lappe Nordic Ski Centre**. The 11K are designed for racing but they can also be enjoyed by the casual skier. Trails are groomed daily. Take Dawson Road west to Dog Lake Road, then two miles west on Concession 4 Road. The large chalet offers food, showers and even a sauna. Fee box at chalet. Phone (807) 623-3735.

Fifteen miles east of Thunder Bay along Highway 11/17 you'll find the **Eldorado Ski Center**. This is a haven for traditional skiing, with 10K of diagonal-only trails for beginning to intermediate skiers. There are no onsite services. Phone (807) 346-8806.

Head farther past Thunder Bay to **Sleeping Giant Provincial Park** for 50K of intermediate to advanced trails. This is classic ski touring country, with long trails through the Sibley Peninsula's deep wilderness of inland lakes, deep valleys and rolling hills. Access all trails through the visitors center. Fee box at trailhead and visitors center. Phone (807) 475-7081.

FOR MORE INFORMATION
Thunder Bay Nordic Trails (807) 475-7081
Snowphone (807) 625-5075

Exploring North Shore Rivers

The North Shore in winter offers a select few experiences that push the boundaries of common sense and, in return, offer extraordinary rewards. There aren't major mountains to conquer, and even the foolish stay off of Lake Superior in the winter. But skiing or snowshoeing on a North Shore river is a peak experience that is available with minimal equipment and only moderate, measurable risk.

Traveling on frozen rivers does involve a substantially greater risk than skiing on groomed trails. There are elements of danger beyond your control. You will have to be prepared to fix accidents in addition to avoiding accidents in the first place.

The rivers of the North Shore are, in winter, snowy paths through an apparent wilderness. Because of zoning laws, even a creek in the middle of Duluth can have a remote feel, with few if any visible intrusions like houses or roads. Travel a river farther up the shore and you are almost guaranteed seclusion. You will get no grand, sweeping views, but rather an intimate sense of the deep winter environment. Signs of animals are everywhere, and watch as you turn each corner for a fleeting glimpse of an otter or a wolf.

The actual beds of rivers are public property. So as long as you stay on the river itself, you may legally go anywhere you want (or can). As soon as you step on shore you could be trespassing.

CHOOSING A SAFE RIVER FOR TRAVEL

The typical North Shore river has a varied character. The roaring cascades and falls seen in state parks like Gooseberry, Tettegouche and Cascade are really the exception to the rule. Approximately 80–90% of the length of a typical North Shore river is relatively flat. The falls and cascades are the most dangerous part of winter travel, but since they are generally short in length, they can be avoided by traveling on land, as if you were portaging a canoe around a rapids.

When choosing a river, look for your safety outlets. If something goes wrong, is there any way out besides the way you came in? If someone falls through the ice and gets soaked, it would be nice to know if there is a house or highway nearby.

Part of choosing safely involves timing. **January and February are the best months for river travel,** since they provide the coldest temperatures and the deepest snow. If you live in the region, watch the weather. A few weeks of deep cold followed by a moderate snowfall can combine for a great river trip.

Check local outing groups for guided trips. The University of Minnesota-Duluth Outdoor Program occasionally offers river ski trips. This kind of guided experience is a great way to learn about river travel if you have never done it before.

EXPLORING A RIVER SAFELY

Traveling safely involves both prior preparation and ongoing vigilance.

Preparation. On any kind of river trip, you should bring additional equipment and clothing specifically to deal with issues of sudden immersion and hypothermia. Breaking through the ice into the near-freezing water below is a real danger and you must be prepared to deal with it.

- **Bring at least one entire extra set of clothes for the group,** especially underwear and socks, and keep them in a waterproof bag in your pack. Chances are if someone does break through, they will only go in a few feet before they catch themselves or, more likely, before they hit bottom. It is critical to get this person into dry clothes immediately, even if it is just dry socks.

- **Bring matches and perhaps a firestarter candle.** If someone goes in all the way, that person will need some external heat like a large, blazing fire.

- **Bring a roomy sleeping bag,** and also keep it in a waterproof bag. A hypothermic person can share the bag with a series of warm people, skin to skin until he or she warms up completely. This is a more reliable and safe way to warm someone up than the blazing fire approach.

- **Bring a rope at least 40 feet long** and keep it within reach at all times. A throw rope designed for whitewater

Animal tracks: "Bounders"

Think long and lean. The North Woods have many long and lean members of the weasel family, and they all leave a distinctive track pattern, a pair of prints nearly side by side but slightly offset. Each set of tracks is between one and three feet away from the next, representing the "bound" of the sinuous animals. This is actually a running gait, with the front feet landing first and the rear feet landing exactly in the prints left by the front feet. The two most common weasels leaving tracks by your ski or snowshoe trail are the pine marten and the fisher. The animals are similar enough in size that their tracks are hard to tell apart; a smaller set would be a marten and a larger set would be a fisher, but there's lots of room in between. Use habitat as a clue: marten are found in the mature boreal forest where they can chase squirrels through the trees. The fisher often captures porcupine and prefers more open successional forest.

paddling works great. This can be tossed to someone who is caught in water.

• **Bring a ski equipment repair kit** (duct tape, replacement ski tip, pocket knife, rope, saw). Compared to skiing on a groomed trail, you're more likely to snap a pole or bust a binding.

• **Bring a friend with you.** Don't try to ski or snowshoe a wilderness river alone. In addition, leave your anticipated travel route with someone back home, along with your estimated time of return.

In order to get someone out of the water, he or she may have to remove skis or snowshoes in order to get legs out. That is okay. It is better to lose a set of skis than lose your life or endanger others.

PICKING YOUR ROUTE

Traveling on a river requires constant vigilance for picking out your route. Roiling open water is still common in the deep of winter. It is generally safer to stay to one side of the river, where the water is shallower and the current generally slower. But avoid the outside of large curves in the river, especially if there is a steep bank above the curve: the water below will likely be deep and fast.

One of the best clues is the tracks of other people, especially if the tracks are fresh. Chances are if the ice held for them it will hold for you, especially if you are traveling the same way (via skis or on snowshoes).

When you get to a waterfall, use your judgement. If it is a deep gorge, go around it completely and avoid getting trapped. If it is an open falls frozen over and snowed over like a ski slope, it may be skiable. Don't ski on ice—leave that for the ice climbers. If you can see the river water moving behind the ice and snow, avoid that area completely.

RECOMMENDED ROUTES

FOR FIRST-TIME RIVER SKIERS

- **Sucker River,** Duluth Township. Park by the bridge on the Old North Shore Road just north of the Highway 61 expressway. This is a mostly level route with a few steep but safe falls.

- **Knife River.** You can access the Knife from the Superior Hiking Trail trailhead in the town of Knife River. It is a flat and easy river, especially above the Highway 61 expressway.

- **Temperance River.** Explore the quiet middle stretch of the Temperance. The river crosses and parallels the Sawbill Trail from the intersection with County Road 1 (about four miles up from Highway 61) all the way to Sawbill Lake.

INTERMEDIATE

- **Amity Creek and Lester River,** Duluth. Amity Creek is tributary to the Lester River, accessible along Seven Bridges Road. For safety, ski above the first bridge and above the big falls. The Lester River is a little larger and is accessible from Lester River Road.

- **Gooseberry River,** above Fifth Falls. If skiing, head up on any of the ski trails. Otherwise, use the Superior Hiking Trail to get above Fifth Falls on land. Then it is easy going for miles.

- **Split Rock River.** Park at wayside rest/Superior Hiking Trail trailhead at the west end of Split Rock Lighthouse State Park. You can go on the hiking trail one way and back on the river, or vice-versa.

ADVANCED

- **Manitou River.** Shuttle cars so you can ski one-way from the junction of County Road 7 with the Manitou River. Use the state park map for navigation. There is a large falls about 2 miles in. The total distance is around seven miles. Exit on the west side of the river before the dangerous falls by Highway 61, and to avoid private property.

- **Devil Track River.** For a full day, pick up the Little Devil Track or the Devil Track itself on the Gunflint Trail and head down through the deep canyon to Lake Superior.

- **Onion River.** Park at the Ray Berglund wayside rest just east of the river.

- **Beaver River.** Park at lot on east side of Beaver Bay. The first mile is the trickiest.

- **Two Island River.** Park on either side of Highway 61 near Taconite Harbor.

- **Brule River** (a.k.a. Arrowhead River). Access the Brule in Judge C.R. Magney State Park. Watch out for the Devil's Kettle!

- **Cascade River**. Shuttle up to County Road 45 and ski down to Highway 61 in Cascade River State Park. The Superior Hiking Trail follows both sides of the river, so you have an out anytime you want. Watch out for the cascades near the end.

Due to fast currents, the Cross River is not recommended. Even more challenging terrain is out there, but it requires technical skills and safety equipment such as helmets, climbing rope and ice augers. For instruction in ice climbing, contact Alpamayo Exploration and Adventure Services in Thunder Bay, (807) 344-9636.

Snowshoeing the North Shore's Winter Woods

Humans are not built for winter. Our bare skin makes us quite vulnerable to cold. To stay warm we have to put on layers of clothing. Similarly, our small feet in comparison with our large bodies make traveling through deep snow nearly impossible.

We have the weight to foot surface-area ratio of a deer, but have only two legs instead of four. And our legs are not nearly as strong and flexible as the deer's. So we often employ one of the deer's techniques for dealing with deep snow: we compress the snow along common routes. A well-trodden path to the outhouse looks quite similar to a deer trail.

But we also employ the techniques of the wolf, hare and grouse: we use snowshoes. By spreading our weight over a larger surface area we don't sink as far in the snow.

Most of us now are beyond the raw necessity of winter travel that led to the invention of snowshoes. We don't have to hunt for our food in January or trek through the woods to check our traplines. Instead, we choose a form of recreation for which the snowshoe is a helpful tool. Some people speak of going snowshoeing as if the tricky strapping on of equipment and the awkward tramping were the end in itself. But those minor hassles are means to an end. Snowshoes are a tool which enable a quiet trek through a wintry land.

Snowshoeing is generally a very different experience than skiing. Snowshoes don't glide, so you move one step at a time and can stop and start on a moment's notice. This allows you to tune in with the environment much more so than you can on skis. Also, with the right snowshoes you can easily go where there is no packed trail—you can follow your curiosity almost wherever it leads you. A few feet of snow make even thick woods quite easy to penetrate and you can wander at will.

Snowshoes have an ancient history in snowbound cultures. They were first developed in northcentral Asia approximately 5000 years ago and were spread east and west through northern cultures from there. Evidence of snowshoe use is found in Finland and Sweden from 4500 years ago. Viking sagas refer to snowshoe use around the year 1000, and during the Norwegian civil war in 1206, King Sverre sent scouts on snowshoes to carry his son to safety over the mountains; the scouts wore birch bark on their legs for warmth, and their route is now the *Birkebinnerrennet* or "birch leg race" for cross-country skiers.

Snowshoe use was also common among native people of North America. In fact, snowshoes are more typical of North America, while skis are more typical of Europe and Asia. Evidence of snowshoe use in the new world goes as far back as the year 1000. The Athapascan people used what is known now as a "bearpaw" style snowshoe. Plains Indians used snowshoes to help hunt buffalo and held a special ceremonial dance for snowshoeing at the beginning of winter. The one native people most closely associated with winter, the Eskimo, have little need for snowshoes. Their snow was and is a windblown crust or sea ice easily covered on foot alone.

EQUIPMENT

Snowshoes. The basic (and only truly necessary) piece of equipment for snowshoeing is, of course, a pair of snowshoes. The purpose of the snowshoe is to distribute your weight so that you do not sink as far into the snow. The increase in surface area is accomplished through lightweight material such as neoprene or rawhide spread over a frame made of wood, plastic or metal.

Some snowshoers (and snowshoe retailers) will fascinate you with the endless varieties of snowshoe styles and the combinations thereof. Are you looking for a Green Mountain style bearpaw? Can you tell the difference between a Michigan and a Maine? Instead of memorizing a dichotomous key of snowshoe types, stick to some basics:

Be wise to size. The softer and fluffier the snow you will be on, the more snowshoe surface area you will need to stay "afloat." You may be surprised by how small a snowshoe you might really need. If you are going into deep woods in the middle of winter after a big snowfall, on trails no one has touched or off trails completely, you will want a bigger snowshoe. If you will be one of ten or twenty snowshoers on the trail that day or even week, a smaller snowshoe will suffice.

Shape matters, a little. Longer, skinnier snowshoes "track" better—they'll keep you going forward well and are good for open country. Shorter, rounder snowshoes maneuver well, and are well-suited for bushwhacking through forests. Snowshoes that are bent up at the toe are easier to walk in, because the tip is less likely to catch on the snow. A pointed tail will act like the keel of a canoe and keep your snowshoe pointed forward.

Bindings matter, a lot. You can choose between a range of bindings. The traditional "H" style leather binding provides excellent control and a snug, customized fit which can require a lot of bare fingered tweaking. The inner tube binding, either handmade from actual inner tube or crafted specially, is an excellent choice for the casual snowshoer: it is easy to put on, and is secure once on, but you will sacrifice some control of the snowshoe. Another binding incorporates a flexible laced-in plastic toe holder with a heel strap; these are a good compromise between ease of use and firmness of control.

The material of the snowshoe is a matter of maintenance and aesthetics. Wood frames with rawhide webbing require the most maintenance but provide a flexibility and "feel" unmatched by the metal and plastic varieties. The high-tech metal and plastic snowshoes provide lightness and ease of use and maintenance.

If you find yourself on the shore without equipment, visit one of the following businesses that rent snowshoes:

- North Star Bikes and Boards, 4521 E. Superior Street, Duluth
- Gowdy's Bed and Breakfast, near Gooseberry Falls State Park
- Tettegouche State Park (for use in park only)
- Lutsen Resort
- Cascade Lodge

Or you can wait for one of the organized group events at Gooseberry Falls State Park or Jay Cooke State Park, using the park's snowshoes. Hartley Nature Center in Duluth offers winter hikes with their set of snowshoes (call 218-724-6735 for information) and so does the Superior Hiking Trail Association (call 218-834-2700).

You may find additional equipment useful for snowshoeing including mukluks, gaiters and ski poles.

Mukluks are the footwear of choice for snowshoeing. They provide an ideal combination of lightness, flexibility and warmth. They also make securing snowshoe bindings very easy. Boots with a removable felt liner will work, but not as well.

Because you will likely be in deeper, looser snow than you might find on a groomed ski trail, you must be more concerned about snow getting into your clothes and boots and then melting there. **Gaiters** which fit over your boots become very useful. And some sort of water resistant (not necessarily waterproof) pants will keep you drier.

When snowshoeing in rugged terrain, especially with a heavy pack, some snowshoers like to have a pair of **ski poles** to help keep their balance. Downhill-length ski poles work better than cross-country-length, but they will need to have a larger basket than most poles.

TECHNIQUE

Words cannot easily describe how to walk with snowshoes. It is a little like learning to walk all over again, except you will accomplish in ten minutes what took six months the first

Downy woodpecker

The birds you'll see

There are over 80 birds known to live in this area year-round. The following are the most common ones you are likely to see on a full day outing:

• Black-capped chickadee
• Raven
• Ruffed grouse
• Downy woodpecker
• Red-breasted nuthatch
• Pine grosbeak

To this list you can add owls. You might see either Barred, Great Horned, Boreal or Saw-whet owls.

Then, depending on where you are, you could easily see some of these:

• Blue jay (oak and pine woods)
• Gray jay (in coniferous forests)
• Bald eagle (near Lake Superior)
• Hairy woodpecker
• Herring gull (on Lake Superior)

Finally, depending on the year, you could see dozens or even hundreds of these "invasive" birds (birds which move about in large flocks in search of food):

• Common redpoll
• Pine siskin
• Bohemian waxwing
• Crossbill, either white-winged or red ❄

Animal tracks: "Hoppers"

If the front legs are in back and the back legs are in front...which way is forwards? Animals such as the snowshoe hare, deer mouse and red squirrel are hoppers, and their tracks show an unusual pattern. After an animal hops, it lands first on its front feet. Then its back feet come down *in front* of the front feet. The faster the hopper goes, the further in front of the front feet do the back feet land. The snowshoe hare track is found near areas with thick underbrush; the much smaller red squirrel track generally runs from tree to tree in coniferous forests. You can always tell which way a hopper was headed; just think backwards. ❅

time. When snowshoeing, you have to think about both the length of your stride (how far forward you move with each step) and the width of your stride (how far apart each step is from an imaginary center line). Walking with snowshoes requires a slightly broader stride than walking or skiing. Once you get walking, the tapered design of most snowshoes allows you to narrow your stride as it gets longer.

As you first head out on snowshoes, you will probably take a few spills. That's okay! It's the way you learn what you can and cannot yet do. You will probably find that getting back up on your feet is tricky. It helps to get your feet downhill from you before attempting to get back up.

As you gain experience and get into more varied terrain, you will find your technique changing depending on whether you are going on the flats or up or down hills. On uphills you may find a herringbone technique helpful, similar to that used when climbing hills on skis. A downhill through deep snow can become a controlled (more or less) glide, or a bounding stride that makes you feel like you are walking on sand dunes on the moon.

SNOWSHOEING ON THE SUPERIOR HIKING TRAIL (SHT)

In the winter, don't think of it as the Superior Hiking Trail anymore. Think of it as the Superior Snowshoeing Area. In the summer you can see the trail on the ground and in the cleared brush. In the winter all you may see is deep snow and the very occasional SHT assurance marker. That's because the SHT passes through open woods like maple and birch and also through open fields. You'll want to have good trail maps, a compass and lots of common sense when you take off on the SHT for a long-distance trek. Even then, you can only expect to be near the SHT, not always on it.

The entire Superior Hiking Trail is available for snowshoeing. Some sections work better than others because of factors like parking and other uses of the trail. Snowshoeing is slower than walking: plan on covering only one mile an hour, less in deep, untracked snow.

Trailhead parking is an issue in winter since many of the smaller SHT parking lots are not plowed. Leaving your car on the side of the road for a few hours can be okay, but overnight parking could invite trouble from snowplows or logging trucks.

Many SHT trailheads are also cross-country skiing trailheads. This likely means that you will be sharing the trail for the first part of your snowshoe trek with skiers who may not think you belong on "their" trail. But as long as you are on a signed route of the SHT, you are fine.

When snowshoeing on a groomed ski trail, either stay on the ungroomed snow at the edge of the track or, if a skate skiing lane exists and the snow is firm, snowshoe there. Do not snowshoe in or near the diagonal skiing lane or lanes.

Below are brief descriptions of the SHT trailheads and the trail between them in winter. For detailed information on trail access and routes, refer to *The Guide to the Superior Hiking Trail,* available from the Superior Hiking Trail Association. Plan your SHT snowshoe outing carefully.

SUPERIOR HIKING TRAIL ACCESS

- **Knife River section (3.6 miles).** In winter, access this section from the wayside rest off of the Highway 61 expressway. The trail winds along the east bank of the Knife River to the Anderson Road (County Road 3).

- **Two Harbors to Castle Danger (9.3 miles).** Access this section from the east end, with the parking lot on Silver Creek 617 off County Road 106 and go west into the rugged ridge overlooking the Silver Creek valley. The Two Harbors end of this trail section is not recommended, since it is shared with snowmobiles and there is only roadside parking.

- **Castle Danger to Gooseberry Falls State Park (8.5 miles).** Take Lake County Road 106 from Castle Danger (turn at the Rustic Inn). This turns into Township Road 617. Take this to the plowed parking lot on the right side. The trail starts with a challenging climb to the top of Wolf Rock. The west half of this section is rolling hills, the eastern half follows the banks of the Gooseberry River down into the state park.

- **Gooseberry Falls State Park to Split Rock River (6.0 miles).** Park at the Gooseberry Visitor Center, cross the Gooseberry River and head up along the east side ski trails that share the way with the SHT for the first 1.2 miles. The trail passes open terrain and two overlooks before descending to the Split Rock River.

- **Split Rock River to Beaver Bay (14.0 miles).** Park at the Split Rock River wayside, on the west side of the river, to access the 4.4 mile Split Rock loop. Or head from either the wayside or the state park's trail center for the long haul to Beaver Bay along dramatic terrain of Christmas Tree and Fault Line ridges.

- **Beaver Bay to Silver Bay (4.7 miles).** The parking lot on County Road 4, 1/2 mile north of Beaver Bay, is plowed occasionally. Otherwise park at the Silver Bay end. This relatively short section takes you past some nice views and piney ridge tops into the land of taconite mining. You'll cross the pipes leading to Milepost Seven and the train tracks bringing the taconite down to the plant in Silver Bay.

- **Silver Bay to Tettegouche State Park/Highway 1 (10.7 miles).** Take Outer Drive from Highway 61 through Silver Bay to Penn Boulevard and the parking lot on the left, which is kept open in winter. This is some of the most dramatic terrain in the western part of the SHT. Bean and Bear Lakes are mountainlike in their grandeur, while Mount Trudee provides sweeping inland views.

- **Highway 1 to County Road 6 (6.8 miles).** There is no plowed parking on this section, so either start at Tettegouche State Park or park along the roadside. This section varies from long level hikes along ridgelines to steep descents into the valleys. There are nice sets of overlooks a mile in from both the west and east ends. These are great destinations for a shorter snowshoe trek.

- **Section 13 (2.2 miles).** Park on the side of the highway. Head uphill through maple woods for some great views from the cliff top. Keep going past the first view to even better ones ahead. There may be ropes put in place to help you up the steep parts. This section dead ends at private property, then picks up again for three miles entering Crosby-Manitou State Park, where parking is also available.

- **Crosby-Manitou State Park to Caribou River (8.1 miles).** Take County Road 7 (Cramer Road) from Finland eight miles to park entrance on right. Park at end of plowed road. This is a dramatic trek through a variety of terrain, including the rugged Manitou River valley and Horseshoe Ridge.

- **Caribou River to County Road 1 (9.0 miles).** If the Caribou River wayside rest is plowed, that's your entrance point to this beautiful gorge. Otherwise there is only roadside parking in winter. After ascending the river valley past the gorge of the Caribou, the trail enters open terrain and birch forests. Sugarloaf Road cuts the section nearly in two; the eastern half skirts Alfred's Pond.

- **County Road 1 to Temperance River (8.0 miles).** Parking is available midway in this section at the Skou Road trailhead, across from the gas station in Schroeder. The western half of this section leads past marsh and an overlook. The trail follows the Cross River for over a mile in the middle before descending into the Temperance River valley.

- **Temperance River to Sawbill Trail (4.8 miles).** This section is best known for Carlton Peak at its midpoint. Park at the Temperance River State Park lots on Highway 61 and head up the east side of the river. Carlton Peak is the most dramatic "mountain" on the SHT, with sweeping views in all directions.

- **Sawbill Trail to Onion River (5.7 miles).** Park at the Britton Peak trailhead, which is a favorite for skiers using the Sugarbush system. After quickly climbing Britton Peak itself, you will head out into the maple forest terrain known well by the skiers here; in fact you will cross the ski trail many times. If you've got the energy, head up and over Leveaux Mountain at the east end.

- **Onion River to Lutsen (6.8 miles).** Park at the Oberg Mountain/Onion River trailhead on Forest Road 336. Most snowshoers here are headed around Oberg Mountain, but if you head east you will find the dramatic terrain of Moose Mountain and a snowy saunter through maple woods back to Lutsen. Cut off the last two miles with a dramatic gondola ride down.

- **Lutsen to Caribou Trail (6.4 miles).** Park at the far end of the Lutsen Mountains lot at the entrance to the cross-country trails. You'll follow the groomed trails up to the bridge over the Poplar River; from there head away from the river for four miles of valley snowshoeing before climbing to an overlook and then descending into the Lake Agnes area.

- **Caribou Trail to Cascade River State Park (9.4 miles).** Park on the roadside at the Caribou Trail end. This is a true ridgeline hike, along the edges of some classic, un-named Sawtooth Mountains. The views are spectacular, especially of the inland valleys.

- **Cascade River State Park to Bally Creek Road (9.5 miles).** Parking is available at either end, in Cascade State Park and on Bally Creek Road (via County Roads 7 and 158). Head up the deeply snowed valley of the Cascade River, on either the west or east side. Once you reach County Road 45, you can either trek on to Bally Creek Road or return on the other side. For a full winter adventure, swap equipment at the Bally Creek Road trailhead and ski down through the Bear Track trails back to Cascade State Park.

- **Bally Creek Road to Grand Marais (8.1 miles).** Park at either end of this section. For the Bally Creek trailhead, head up County Road 7 to Forest Road 158 and take this nearly to the end of the plowed road, a trailhead shared with the Bear Track trails. It's a deep woods snow-shoe in red pine and cedar all the way through to Pincushion Mountain above Grand Marais, except for the last stretch through a marsh, which is shared with a snowmobile trail.

- **Grand Marais to County Road 58 (4.7 miles).** From the Pincushion trailhead off the Gunflint Trail just above Grand Marais, head along the combined SHT/Pincushion Mountain ski trails onto the Pincushion Mountain loop. Watch for the sign that points hikers off the ski trail and down into the rugged valley of the Devils Track River. You'll cross the river, climb again, then head along the valley's edge to the end.

- **County Road 58 to Kadunce River (9.2 miles).** An otherwise routinely fun winter hike can become spectacular with a trek up the Kadunce River gorge. See Exploring North Shore Rivers (page 143) for safety information and be prepared for a potentially dangerous outing. Only roadside parking is available in winter on County Road 58.

- **Kadunce River to Magney (10.0 miles).** From the way-side rest at the Kadunce River, head up the SHT spur and onto a quick two mile loop back to the lakeshore, where for 1.6 miles you can snowshoe the beach on Lake Superior. Then head inland with some views of Lake Superior before reaching Judge C.R. Magney State Park, where you will share the last mile of trail with skiers.

- **Judge C.R. Magney State Park to Arrowhead Trail (4.3 miles completed).** From the parking lot at the state park, head past Devil's Kettle through old growth hardwoods to County Road 69.

- **Arrowhead Trail to Jackson Lake Road (5.1 miles).** From the roadside parking on the Arrowhead Trail (County Road 16) head along a remote and rugged ridgeline with lots of views the entire route, including views of Isle Royale.

- **Jackson Lake Road to Canada (8.7 miles).** Only roadside parking is available at both ends. This is the end of the SHT, passing through remote northern forest and logged areas and around scenic Jackson Lake.

OTHER RECOMMENDED ROUTES

There are many other places to snowshoe along the North Shore. The following list will get you started, but explore around and see what else you can find.

DULUTH-SUPERIOR

- **Jay Cooke State Park.** The park signs and maintains snowshoe trails in two large loops that start and end in the campground area across from the visitors center. Also try the Grand Portage Trail at the east end of the park and the Carlton Trail on the other side of the river at the west end of the park.

- **Wisconsin Point.** Follow the signs from U.S. Highway 2 to this windswept and more wild companion to Minnesota Point. The marshes of Allouez Bay provide wide open (and deeply snowed) room to roam. Watch for signs of moose here.

- **Duluth City Parks.** Winter recreation in Duluth's city parks is not limited to skiing. You should not snowshoe on the groomed ski trails, but the following parks have opportunities for snowshoeing: **Mission Creek Trail,** in Fond du Lac; **Enger Tower,** along the overlook trails; **Chester Creek,** below Skyline Drive; and **Lester Park**, in the hiking trails near the pagoda and playground area.

- **Hawk Ridge trails.** Take Skyline Drive east from Glenwood or west from Seven Bridges Road and head off anywhere into the hills.

- **Minnesota Point.** Once you are beyond the airport, the pine woods and open meadows are ideal for winter tramping.

LAKE COUNTY

- **Knife River.** There are some enjoyable trails through white pine marked for hiking and skiing right off of scenic Old Highway 61 on the west side of the Knife River.

- **Woodland Caribou Trail.** Thirty-eight miles north of Two Harbors on County Highway 2 you will find this vast spread of wilderness trail. There are twenty miles of trail in mostly level terrain around small lakes. Although listed in older publications as a ski trail, this is best suited for snowshoes.

- **Gooseberry Falls State Park.** Snowshoeing is allowed everywhere in the park, including the ski trails (but don't disturb the track). The Voyageur and Fifth Falls Trail is a hiking-only loop that takes you from Highway 61 across the Fifth Falls bridge and back down the other side.

- **Split Rock Lighthouse State Park.** Try the Day Hill trails, including climb to summit, but watch out at the stairs. Or just walk around the Campground trails. The Split Rock River loop is part of the SHT and is an excellent long trek.

- **Twin Lakes Trail.** From the Bay Area Historical Society parking lot in Silver Bay, take this 4.2 mile "lollipop loop" to Bean and Bear Lakes, including a section of the SHT.

- **Tettegouche State Park.** From the trailhead parking lot inside the park, take the SHT east to High Falls or west to Raven Rock. From the wayside rest, take the Shovel Point trail (often tracked and packed by hikers but good snowshoeing after big snows) or the High Falls along the east side of the Baptism. Snowshoes are available for rent at the park office, for $6 per day.

- **Crosby-Manitou State Park.** The whole park offers excellent snowshoeing and winter camping. Secure your camping permit back at Tettegouche then head out on any of the trails. The upper trails are marked as ski trails, but few people ski them. Bensen Lake has a quiet feel, but deep in the Manitou River gorge you will feel far removed from civilization.

COOK COUNTY

- **Temperance River State Park.** If you are up for a big trek, take the SHT to Carlton Peak and return. Otherwise, poke around on the trails on the east side of the river (these used to be ski trails), like the Inner Hidden Falls and Cauldron Trail.

- **Britton Peak.** Park with the skiers and head up the SHT for the quick trek to Britton Peak along the SHT. This is an easily accessible, often-traveled route. Or bushwhack in the open maple woods of the first beginner loop—you won't get lost if you stay within the ski trails.

- **Oberg Mountain.** From the Onion River trailhead, take this scenic loop around the maple woods on top of Oberg.

- **Cascade State Park.** On the west side of the river, from Cascade Lodge, take any of the trails between Cascade Creek and Cascade River. Although some of these are marked for skiing, they are multiuse and better suited for snowshoeing. Also, take the SHT to the top of Lookout Mountain and return along the Lookout Mountain Trail. On the east side of the river, you can snowshoe around the picnic area or just take off in the cedar woods (watch for deer and wolf sign).

GUNFLINT TRAIL

- **George Washington Pines.** This loop is open to skiing and snowshoeing, and is a great introduction to either.

- **Central Gunflint.** Golden Eagle Lodge and Bearskin Lodge offer snowshoe outings to their guests on nearby trails to scenic ridge tops.

- **Upper Gunflint.** Try parts of the Kekekabic Trail or any of the lake-and-portage combinations of the BWCA.

GRAND MARAIS TO THUNDER BAY

- **Judge C.R. Magney State Park.** From the far parking lot, cross the Brule River and head up the SHT past Lower and Upper Falls to Devil's Kettle.

- Take the **Grand Portage** itself nine miles in to Fort Charlotte on the Pigeon River.

BUSHWHACKING

When there is a few feet of snow on the ground and you've got some off-trail snowshoes, who needs a trail? With a map and compass, the whole forest is your trail.

Find a good topographic map for your chosen bushwhacking area. Take a compass bearing on a ridge or waterfalls or other landmark. Follow this compass bearing through the woods, over hills, across frozen beaver ponds, around cliffs, past soaring trees and remote animal dens. You're bound to find wonderful surprises and a feeling of adventure as you boldly go where, as far as you can tell, no one has gone before.

If you aren't comfortable with map and compass, find some part of a state park or ski trailhead that is surrounded by a loop of a ski trail. The ski trail becomes your boundary marker. Stay within the ski trail and you can't get too lost.

Snowshoeing is rightly becoming a popular way to enjoy the winter woods. More than skiing, it is a chance to truly immerse in nature and let your childlike spirit of adventure take over. Just stay warm and stay out of the ski trail!

Photo: RUDI HARGESHEIMER

Other Winter Fun
along the North Shore

There are countless ways to celebrate and experience a North Shore winter. Stir together the sometimes raging seas of Lake Superior with the shimmering cold and deep snow of the North Woods and all sorts of magic can emerge. Let the child with you or within you "come out and play."

Below you will find dozens of places and ideas for winter fun. This is not a complete listing—let your imagination soar, and let us know what else you find!

STORM WATCHING

Winter storms on Lake Superior provide one of the most humbling experiences around. In a major storm, the lake is so powerful and the wind so strong that you feel like dust on a feather. November is the month most associated with storms, especially the "northeasters" that settle in for a day or more. But northeasters can come in any month.

How to have a blast. To best experience a roaring northeaster, find a promontory that faces "up" the shore, i.e. northeast. Dress more warmly than you expect to dress: wind protection for both legs and torso, neckwarmer, mittens and sunglasses. The wind chill could easily be many degrees below zero, and you will want to stay out in the blast for at least ten minutes. Stand in a secure area just close enough to the breaking waves that you can smell the water but not be doused by it. Shifting winds can blow you off your feet, so do not stand where one false step could spell doom.

Where to have a blast. Many of the state parks provide great storm watching. Specifically, try:

- **Agate Beach** and the picnic area at **Gooseberry Falls State Park.**

- **Shovel Point** at **Tettegouche State Park** (the ten minute walk in will warm you up).

- Highway 61 parking area at **Cascade River State Park.**

Other storm watching sites include:

- **Duluth's Lakewalk** and **Canal Park** area near the aerial lift bridge and ship canal piers (piers are closed in winter).

- **Stoney Point.**

- **Artist's Point,** Grand Marais.

- For a slightly more sedate experience, try the Bridge restaurant at **Bluefin Bay** in Tofte, where you can sip coffee and watch the breakers. You can also feel them as they crash. All you will miss is the smell and the chill.

EXPERIENCING LAKE SUPERIOR ICE

In the winter of 1993–94 Lake Superior froze over completely. This is supposed to happen only every fifteen years or so. Two years later, it happened again. So, despite gloomy predictions of global warming, Lake Superior seems to be inviting more and more people to sample its winter treasures. Be careful. **Lake Superior freezing is nothing like other lakes.** The wind moves chunks of ice the size of Lake Mille Lacs around as if it were a shuffleboard player. While you are out walking, you might unexpectedly be on your way to Michigan.

When the ice is just right...

You can lay face down and pick out fish below. When the wind and temperature are right, the whole ice mass can sing like sounding whales. And with a strong wind the ice piles up with a hiss on and near shore in little glimmering mountains. ❄

However…when the ice has settled in just right, it can be up to four feet thick and clearer than fine glass, with beautiful joints and pressure fractures coursing through like quartz veins. You can lie face down and pick out fish below. When the wind and temperature are right, the whole ice mass can sing like sounding whales. And, with a strong wind, the ice piles up with a hiss on and near shore in glimmering little mountains. You can witness plate tectonics in action as little San Andreas faults rip apart the ice sheet.

The ice watching action is best in February and March when, according to Lake Superior's weird rules, the water is at its coldest. Almost every year there is some freezing, especially in protected bays. Come and catch the everchanging show.

SNOWCRUST WALKING

Another ephemeral wonder is the spring thaw crust. During the first good thaw of the spring, when temperatures stay at or above freezing for at least a day, the top few feet of snow partially melt and the crystals metamorphose. When the temperature inevitably drops again, all these mushy metamorphosed crystals freeze into a solid mass. The end result of this is a crust that is hard as cement.

With this crust, for a few days or weeks you do not need snowshoes or even skis to get around in the woods. Instead, you can simply walk on your own feet. You will probably break through the crust every once in a while, especially where there is heavy undergrowth, but for the most part you can cruise wherever you want. **Watch the weather reports for a good thaw followed by a deep freeze.** It can be as early as January and as late as April. Put two inches of fresh snow on top, get your "beater" skis on and take off into the woods.

DOGSLEDDING

It used to be that dogsledding was only available to a few hardcore racers. Now, with the sport growing by fuzzy leaps and husky bounds, virtually anyone can enjoy it. There are numerous mushers along the North Shore who can take you out for an hour, a day or a week. Contact Arleigh Jorgenson at Silver Creek Kennels (218) 387-2498 or Boundary Country Trekking at (800) 322-8327. Many of the larger resorts, especially on the Gunflint Trail, offer onsite dogsledding.

You can also be a spectator to one of the best sled dog races in the country, the John Beargrease Sled Dog Marathon. If you know when the mushers are coming through, you could time your backcountry outing to intersect (but not to go on) the Beargrease trail and cheer the teams on.

SKIJORING

This hybrid of dog mushing and cross-country skiing is gaining in popularity as well, especially among those who love sled dogs but only want to keep one or a few of them. Skijorers harness one or two sled dogs and connect themselves to the dog with a wide padded waist belt. Then, with the human on skis, dog and human sprint along together. A quick release hitch on the connecting gangline is a lifesaver if the dog takes off after a squirrel. The skijorer either skate skis or diagonal skis, sharing the load with the dog. Contact the Duluth Pack Store in Duluth, (218) 722-1707, for more information on equipment.

ANIMAL TRACKING

The art of tracking animals in winter is a true form of natural history, that is, using signs in the snow to tell stories of life in the woods. It is well worth buying a guide to animal tracks and learning how to read these stories. Knowing that you are sharing the trail with a wolf or moose sends primordial chills down the spine. Some recommended tracking books are listed at the end of this book.

WINTER CAMPING AND SLEEPING OUTSIDE

Winter camping is a wonderful experience when you are properly prepared. This book won't go into depth on how to winter camp; there are some excellent and thorough books on the subject you can read before heading out (see Resources chapter).

Sleeping outside on a cold winter's night is not only for backcountry adventurers. It can also be a great experience for those staying in a lodge or cabin. Get a quality sleeping bag rated to at least -20°F and some foam pads to sleep on and to insulate you from the cold of the snow. Set all this up on a waterproof ground cloth, and climb on in. You may not sleep all that well, but the crystalline stars and hooting of owls make it worthwhile. If you are looking for someplace to go, one hint is that most of the state parks along the North Shore have winter campsites.

If you are on the Superior Hiking Trail, you should know that the Superior Hiking Trail Association strongly recommends camping at designated campsites year around. These sites are typically well suited for winter camping, as they are down in the river valleys, well protected from winter wind and with plenty of snow for building shelters. Most of these sites are quite near running water for drinking and cooking; as in the summer, water should be treated before use. Also, be extra careful in drawing water from wintery streams; falling in is easier and more hazardous than in summer.

If you choose to camp elsewhere than a designated campsite, be sure it is not private land and not in a state park, as camping in those places would be illegal.

INN-TO-INN AND HUT-TO-HUT

If you really want to ski and feel like you have accomplished something, try skiing inn-to-inn or hut-to-hut. Cooperating lodging establishments along the North Shore and the Gunflint Trail offer well organized package deals. Ski from one resort to the next with a lunch packed especially for you. The adventurous can throw a night in a yurt or remote cabin into the mix. Your luggage will be shuttled for you. Packages from two nights to four nights and more are available in both areas, as well as the excellent Pincushion Mountain system. Boundary Country Trekking coordinates all these options. See the Resources chapter for more information.

DOWNHILL SKIING

If you thrill more to the downhill glide than the uphill grind, you have a number of opportunities on the North Shore to let a chairlift do the work for you. Break up a week long winter cross-country vacation with a wild day at Lutsen Mountain or Spirit Mountain; diehard cross-country skiers can use the excellent trails at both facilities. Take the whole family cheaply to Mont-du-Lac off Highway 23 just past the St. Louis River south of Duluth. In Duluth, check out Chester Bowl, perfect for the beginning skier. If you are committed to cross-country skiing, try a day of telemark skiing and chalk it up to crosstraining for those tight curves on the advanced loop.

CROSS-COUNTRY SKI RACES AND SNOWSHOE RACES

On almost any weekend in January and February there are cross-country ski races somewhere on or near the North Shore.

The **Pincushion Mountain** trails come alive in early January with the running of the Sawtooth International, including a 17K classic race, a 25K freestyle, and junior races from 5K for 14–15 year olds to 100 meters for those age five and under. For more information, call (218) 387-1276.

Superior Municipal Forest is the location for the Superior Ski Classic race, typically held in mid January. The race includes a 15K classic race and 42K and 15K freestyle races. For more information, call (800) 942-5313.

Snowflake Nordic Center hosts many races throughout the season.

Korkki Nordic Ski Center hosts the annual Erik Judeen race in late January, the longest running race in the Northland.

The **Sleeping Giant** trails host the annual Sibley Ski Tour in late winter, with a 50K freestyle race, a 20K race and tour and a 10K tour. For more information, call (807) 475-7081.

ICE FISHING

Hanging out by a hole in the ice hoping for a bite has a certain Zen-like quality to it, especially when you throw in the dimly lit shack and the glow of sunlight back up the hole, diffused by snow, ice and water. Hot fishing spots along the North Shore include Lake Superior off of the French and Lester Rivers, Tettegouche State Park and virtually any of the Boundary Waters lakes off the Gunflint Trail. Check in at the local bait shops for leads or even a local guide. Dogsled outfitters offer day-long Boundary Waters trout fishing excursions to remote wilderness lakes.

SNOWMOBILING

Few sports seem as mutually exclusive as snowmobiling and cross-country skiing. It seems that many snowmobilers have never cross-country skied, and many cross-country skiers have never snowmobiled. Yet the North Shore is a heavenly destination for both sports. You can rent a snowmobile for a day or week at Beaver Bay Sport Shop, (218) 226-4666, or at Castle Danger Sport, (218) 834-4646. Take off onto the 170-mile North Shore State Trail connecting Duluth and Grand Marais. Or ride the Tomahawk Trail eighty miles inland to Ely. You can stop for a bite at any of the inns along the way. Stay on the trails, know the laws, and please do not drink and drive.

SLEDDING

It may be the most universal winter sport. Put a few inches of snow on a hill and out come the sleds, the Flexible Flyers, the food trays and cardboard boxes for endless swoops down the hill and excited walks back up. However, the North Shore is strangely lacking in good sliding areas. The landscape is too young, too wild and too fresh from the glaciers to have the right combination of open hills and safe runout. In the Duluth area, try the public golf courses, Lincoln Park, Leif Erikson Park or the Lester Park chalet. Up the shore, just ask any kid where the sledding hill is!

ICE SKATING

Sharpen up the skates and, with dreams of Wayne Gretsky or Kristi Yamaguchi, head for the nearest patch of ice for a classic winter thrill. The city of Duluth is riddled with twenty-two public skating rinks, from schoolyard squares to hockey rinks complete with lights and boards. In Two Harbors, skate at Odegard Park, on 13th Avenue near the water tower (the "main drag" is 7th Avenue). In Silver Bay, evening skating is available for $1 per person at the Arena, across from the high school. Bluefin Bay in Tofte offers a small lakeside rink for their guests. In Grand Marais, try the rink at the community center.

Skating on local lakes is a matter of great timing. In late November and early December there can be a window between freeze-up of the lakes and the first wet snow. It lasts one week or at most two. Get out and enjoy! For a serious adventure, wait for ideal ice conditions on Lake Superior. Sane people have skated across the lake from Lester River to the Middle River in Wisconsin; this is only feasible on occasional years and certainly only before the shipping lanes are open for traffic.

Resources
for Planning your
North Shore Getaway

When you're coming to the North Shore for a winter vacation, use the following resources to plan and enjoy your trip.

NORTH SHORE CHAMBERS AND ASSOCIATIONS

- Carlton Area Chamber of Commerce
  PO Box 526, Carlton MN 55718

- Cloquet Area Chamber of Commerce
  225 Sunnyside Drive, Cloquet MN 55720
  (218) 879-1551 or (800) 554-4350

- Duluth Convention and Visitors Bureau
  Endion Station, 100 Lake Place Drive
  Duluth MN 55802
  (218) 722-4011 or (800)-4-DULUTH

- Duluth-Superior Motel-Hotel Association
  PO Box 710, Duluth MN 55802

- Lake Superior North Shore Association
  PO Box 159, Duluth MN 55801

- Two Harbors Chamber of Commerce
  603 Seventh Avenue, Two Harbors MN 55616
  (218) 834-2600 or (800) 777-7384

- Lake County Visitor Information Center
  8 Highway 61 East, Two Harbors MN 55616
  (218) 834-4005 or (800) 554-2116

- Beaver Bay Tourism Info Center
  Beaver Bay MN 55601 (218) 226-3317
  (mid-May through mid-September)

- Silver Bay Chamber of Commerce
  Box 26, Silver Bay MN 55614 (218) 226-4044

- Lutsen-Tofte Tourism Association
  Box 2248, Tofte MN 55615
  (218) 663-7804 or (888) 616-6784

- Grand Marais Chamber of Commerce
  PO Box 1048, Grand Marais MN 55604
  (218) 387-2524 or (800) 622-4014

- Tip of the Arrowhead
  Association
  PO Box 1048
  Grand Marais MN 55604
  (218) 387-2524 or
  (800) 622-4014

- Gunflint Trail Association
  PO Box 205
  Grand Marais MN 55604
  (800) 338-6932

- Grand Portage Tourist
  Association
  Box 233
  Grand Portage MN 55605
  (218) 475-2401 or
  (800) 232-1384 USA
  (800) 543-1384 CAN

- North of Superior Tourism
  (Thunder Bay and Ontario)
  1119 Victoria Avenue E.
  Thunder Bay ON
  P7C 1B7 (800) 265-3951

- Tourism Thunder Bay
  500 Donald Street E.
  3rd Floor City Hall
  Thunder Bay ON
  P7E 5V3
  (800) 667-8386

ADDITIONAL TRAVEL AND TOURISM INFORMATION

- Minnesota Office of
  Tourism
  100 Metro Square Building
  121 7th Place East,
  St. Paul MN 55101-2112
  (800) 657-3700 or
  (612) 296-5029

When you want more about the North Shore, reach for this companion book

Guide to the Superior Hiking Trail details over 200 miles of wilderness footpath on the north shore of Lake Superior, running from Two Harbors to the Canadian border. The Superior Hiking Trail weaves along the Sawtooth Mountain range through a region of lush forests, spectacular wildflowers and diverse wildlife. This trail guide provides mile-by-mile information on trailhead access, parking accommodations, designated campsites, scenic overlooks and linkages to the eight Minnesota State Parks along the trail. Complete trail maps are included in each section of the book.

Let this book help you park your car, arrange a shuttle, find water or find a camp. It'll tell you where you're likely to see a moose or to see Isle Royale, where you're treading in the Voyageur's footsteps and why the rock fractures the way it does along the Split Rock river.

$14.95
Superior Hiking Trail Association
PO Box 4, 731 Seventh Avenue
Two Harbors MN 55161
(218) 834-42700

- U.S. Forest Service Tofte Ranger Station
  (218) 663-7280

- U.S. Forest Service Gunflint Ranger District
  (218) 327-1750

- Minnesota Department of Natural Resources
  State Parks information
  500 Lafayette Road, St. Paul MN 55155
  (612) 296-6157 or (800)766-6000
  State Parks reservations (800) 246-2267

NORTH SHORE RELATED ORGANIZATIONS

- Superior Hiking Trail Association
  PO Box 4, Two Harbors MN 55616
  (218) 834-2700

- Sugarloaf Interpretive Center Association
  31 W. Superior Street, #401
  Duluth MN 55802

- John Beargrease Sled Dog Marathon
  600 E. Superior Street, Suite 305
  Duluth MN 55802
  (218) 722-7631

OUTFITTERS, GUIDES

- UMD Outdoor Program (guided trips)
  121 Sports and Health Center
  10 University Drive
  Duluth MN 55812
  (218) 726-6533
  email: outdoor@d.umn.edu

- Boundary Country Trekking (for inn-to-inn and
  hut-to-hut skiing, etc.)
  7925 Gunflint Trail
  Grand Marais MN 55604
  (800) 322-8327 or (218) 388-9972
  email: bct@boreal.org

• Alpamayo Exploration and Adventure Services,
Ltd. (for ice-climbing)
PO Box 2204
Thunder Bay ON P7B 5E8
(807) 344-9636

ROAD CONDITIONS
• Duluth and North Shore (218) 723-4866
• Minnesota statewide (800) 542-0220

RECOMMENDED READING
WINTER ECOLOGY, NATURAL HISTORY AND TRACKING
Halfpenny, James C. and Roy Douglas Ozanne. *Winter: An Ecological Handbook.* Boulder CO: Johnson Books, 1989.

Marchand, Peter. *Life in the Cold.* Hanover NH: University Press of New England, 1991.

Murie, Olaus Johan. *A Field Guide to Animal Tracks.* New York NY: Houghton-Mifflin, 1975.

Stall, Chris. *Animal Tracks of the Great Lakes States.* Seattle WA: Mountaineers Books, 1990.

Stokes, Donald. *A Guide to Nature in Winter.* Boston MA: Little, Brown and Co., 1976.

CROSS-COUNTRY SKIING
Bergan, Sindre and Bob O'Connor. *Cross Country Skiing.* Indianapolis IN: Masters Press, 1997.

Cazeneuve, Brian. *Cross-Country Skiing: A Complete Guide.* New York NY: W.W. Norton and Co., 1995.

Gullion, Laurie. *The Cross-Country Primer.* New York NY: Lyons and Burford, 1990.

Moynier, John. *The Basic Essentials of Cross-Country Skiing.* Merrillville IN: ICS Books, 1990.

Noren, Elizabeth and Gary Noren. *Ski Minnesota.* Minneapolis MN: Nodin Press, 1985.

Wicks, David. *Making Tracks: An Introduction to Cross-Country Skiing*. Boulder CO: Pruett Pub., 1995.

SNOWSHOEING

Edwards, Sally and Melissa McKenzie. *Snowshoeing*. Champaign IL: Human Kinetics Pub.,1995.

Olmsted, Larry. *Snowshoeing: A Trailside Guide*. New York NY: W.W. Norton and Co., 1997.

Prater, Gene. *Snowshoeing*. Seattle, WA: Mountaineers Books, 1988.

Zwosta, Marianne. *The Essential Snowshoer*. New York NY: McGraw-Hill, 1997.

VARIOUS WINTER SKILLS

Conover, Garrett and Alexandra Conover. *A Snow Walkers Companion: Winter Trail Skills for the Far North*. New York NY: McGraw-Hill, 1994.

Lowe, Jeff. *Ice World: Techniques and Experiences of Modern Ice Climbing*. Seattle WA: Mountaineers Books, 1996.

Stark, Peter and Steven Krauzer. *Winter Adventure: A Complete Guide to Winter Sports*. New York NY: W.W. Norton and Co., 1996.

Townsend, Chris. *Wilderness Skiing and Winter Camping*. New York NY: McGraw-Hill, 1996.

FOR KIDS

Bowen, Betsy. *Tracks in the Wild*. Boston MA: Little Brown and Co., 1993.

Trail Update Form

Help us help people enjoy winter! North shore ski trails and other winter opportunities are always changing as new trails get built and old ones fade away. Your eyes and ears can help keep this book up to date.

Maybe you found something in this book that is incorrect. Maybe you stumbled upon a great new trail. Or maybe you found a fun new way to play outside in winter. Please let us know!

Your name _____

Your address _____

Your phone _____

Trail update information

If referencing a page in this book, please give page number _____

Are there other people we can contact for more information about this update?

SEND TO: Winter Guide Update, Superior Hiking Trail Association, PO Box 4, Two Harbors MN 55616

Thanks!

Join the Superior Hiking Trail Association!

APPLICATION FOR MEMBERSHIP OR RENEWAL
Memberships run for one year from receipt of application

Membership Categories

❏ Student/Senior $15

❏ Family $30

❏ Supporting $100

❏ Individual $20

❏ Youth organization/
    Nonprofit $40

❏ Life Member $500

Donation $ _____

CORPORATE

❏ Contributing $50

❏ Supporting $100

❏ Sustaining $500

❏ Patron $1,000

Donation $ _____

Enclosed is $_____ for

❏ New membership

❏ Renewal (member # _____)

Name _____

Address _____

_____

Home phone _____

Work phone _____

The Superior Hiking Trail Association is composed of volunteers.
To accomplish our goals, we need the active involvement of our members.

I am interested in helping the Superior Hiking Trail Association through

❏ Constructing trails

❏ Fundraising

❏ Group presentations

❏ Maintaining trails

❏ Promotion/publicity/marketing

❏ Art/photography

❏ Special skills: _____

❏ Liaison with other organizations

  (name of group) _____

Mail to: Superior Hiking Trail Assn., PO Box 4, Two Harbors MN 55616

Thank you!